CROSSCURRENTS *Modern Critiques*

CROSSCURRENTS *Modern Critiques*
Harry T. Moore, *General Editor*

Norman Kelvin

E. M. Forster

WITH A PREFACE BY
Harry T. Moore

Carbondale and Edwardsville

SOUTHERN ILLINOIS UNIVERSITY PRESS

FEFFER & SIMONS, INC.

London and Amsterdam

To Phyllis

Copyright © 1967 by Southern Illinois University Press
Library of Congress Card Number 67–10282
Printed in the United States of America
Designed by Andor Braun

PREFACE

THE LITERARY STATUS of E. M. Forster has been for many years an unusual one. In his long lifetime (he was born in 1879) he has published only five novels, the last of them as long ago as 1924, yet critics and other readers have long ranked him among those few writers at the top of the contemporary novel. Books about him continue to appear, adding significant new insights or helping to readjust perspectives. The latest of these, by Norman Kelvin, makes its own distinct contribution to the further understanding and appreciation of Forster.

Like all other explicators of Forster, Mr. Kelvin finds the last two of the novels, Howards End (1910) and A Passage to India (1924), superior to the other three; and he points out that there is an eternal argument as to which of the last two is the better. But he also notes the enduring popularity of the other three: Where Angels Fear to Tread (1905), The Longest Journey (1907), and A Room with a View (1908). About twenty years ago these last books seemed fairly fragile and perhaps not destined to last; but they have endured along with the two novels of magnitude. Similarly, Forster's two volumes of short stories, written before World War I and first put into a collected edition in 1947, have lasted, while most of his nonfiction work—ranging from his Alexandria guidebook to literary essays—is readily obtainable. To his many admirers (and as my own small book on him demonstrates, I am among them), Forster's continued success is gratifying, a proof that literary justice certainly exists.

Mr. Kelvin begins his book with what might be called a reasonable biography of Forster, based chiefly on his own references to himself, for the most part in two biographies he has written: Goldsworthy Lowes Dickinson (1934), the story of a Cambridge friend, and Marianne Thornton (1956), Forster's eighteenth-century aunt whom he knew in his childhood. Mr. Kelvin turns next to the short stories, noting that all but two of them deal with fantasy and indicating their additional concern with class distinctions. Then he takes up the novels, in chronological order, in what comprises the heart of his book. He is above all concerned with aspects of Forster's humanism, about which he provides some fresh and valuable observations, along with other generally useful interpretations. He ends his study with a helpful discussion of Forster's ideas.

Before writing this book, Mr. Kelvin—who teaches at the City College of New York—published that fine study, A Troubled Eden: Nature and Society in the Works of George Meredith, brought out in 1961 by Stanford University Press and Oliver and Boyd. He is now preparing an edition of the letters of William Morris. We are happy to have, in the Crosscurrents / Modern Critiques series, Mr. Kelvin's valuable book on E. M. Forster.

HARRY T. MOORE

Southern Illinois University

March 4, 1967

ACKNOWLEDGMENTS

THE AUTHOR and publisher wish to thank Mr. E. M. Forster for permission to quote extensively from his writings and to acknowledge permissions for critical readings which appear in *E. M. Forster*.

The works by E. M. Forster as follows.

Abinger Harvest © 1936 by Edward Arnold Ltd. and © 1936 by Harcourt, Brace & World, Inc. *Aspects of the Novel* © 1927 by Edward Arnold Ltd. and © 1927 by Harcourt, Brace & World, Inc. *Collected Short Stories* © 1947 by Alfred A. Knopf, Inc. and © 1948 by Sidgwick & Jackson Ltd. *Goldsworthy Lowes Dickenson* © 1934 by Edward Arnold Ltd. and © 1934 by Harcourt, Brace & World, Inc. *The Hill of Devi* © 1953 by Harcourt, Brace & World, Inc. *Howards End* © 1910 by Edward Arnold Ltd. and © 1921 by Alfred A. Knopf, Inc. *The Longest Journey* © 1924 by Edward Arnold Ltd. and © 1922 by Alfred A. Knopf, Inc., and © 1960 by Oxford University Press. *Marianne Thornton: A Domestic Biography, 1797–1887* © 1956 by Harcourt, Brace & World, Inc. *A Passage to India* © 1924 by Edward Arnold Ltd. and © 1924 by Harcourt, Brace & World, Inc. *Pharos and Pharillon* © 1923 by The Hogarth Press Ltd. and © 1923 by Alfred A. Knopf, Inc. *A Room with a View* © 1908 by Edward Arnold Ltd. and © 1923 by Alfred A. Knopf, Inc. *Two Cheers for Democracy* © 1951 by Harcourt, Brace & World, Inc. *Where Angels Fear to Tread* © 1924 by Edward Arnold Ltd. and © 1920 by Alfred A. Knopf, Inc.

Books and Articles about E. M. Forster

John Beer, *The Achievement of E. M. Forster* © 1962 by
Chatto & Windus Ltd. F. C. Crews, *E. M. Forster: The
Perils of Humanism* © 1962 by Princeton University
Press. P. N. Furbank and F. J. Haskell, *Writers at Work:
Paris Review Interviews*, ed. Malcolm Cowley © 1957,
1958 by the Paris Review, Inc., reprinted by permission of
The Viking Press, Inc. and Martin Secker & Warburg
Ltd. K. W. Gransden, *E. M. Forster* © 1962 by Grove
Press, Inc., and thanking Oliver & Boyd Ltd. for permis-
sion. K. W. Gransden, "E. M. Forster at Eighty" © 1959
by *Encounter*. James Hall, "Forster's Family Reunions"
© 1958 by *English Literary History*. A. E. Housman, from
"From far, from eve and morning" from "A Shropshire
Lad"—Authorised Edition—from *The Collected Poems of
A. E. Housman*, copyright 1939, 1940 © 1959 by Holt,
Rinehart and Winston, Inc. © 1967 by Robert E. Symons,
reprinted by permission of Holt, Rinehart and Winston,
Inc., and The Society of Authors. Cyrus Hoy, "Forster's
Metaphysical Novel" © 1960 and reprinted by permission
of the Modern Language Association from *PMLA*, LXXV
(1959). J. K. Johnstone, "E. M. Forster," *The Bloomsbury
Group: A Study of E. M. Forster, Lytton Strachey, Vir-
ginia Woolf, and Their Circle* © 1954 by Farrar, Straus &
Giroux, Inc. Arnold Kettle, *An Introduction to the English Novel* © 1951 by Hutchinson Publishing Group Ltd.
and © 1960 by Harper & Row Publishers, Inc. F. R.
Leavis, "E. M. Forster," *The Common Pursuit* © 1952 by
Chatto & Windus Ltd. and by New York University Press.
Frederick McDowell, "The Mild Intellectual Light: Idea
and Theme in *Howards End*" © 1959 and reprinted by
permission of the Modern Language Association from
PMLA, LXXIV (1959). Harry T. Moore, *E. M. Forster* ©
1965 by Columbia University Press. H. J. Oliver, *The Art
of E. M. Forster*, Australian Humanities Research Council
Monograph no. 4 (Melbourne University Press, 1960),

pp. 3–4. V. S. Pritchett, "Mr. Forster's New Year" © 1958 by *New Statesman and Nation.* John Crowe Ransom, "E. M. Forster" © 1943 by *The Kenyon Review.* Lionel Trilling, *E. M. Forster* © 1943 by New Directions Publishing Corporation and © 1944 by The Hogarth Press Ltd. Alan Wilde, *Art and Order: A Study of E. M. Forster* © 1964 by New York University Press. Angus Wilson, "The Revolt of Samuel Butler © 1957 by The Atlantic Monthly Company, Boston, Mass. Reprinted with permission.

CONTENTS

E. M. Forster

1   INTRODUCTION

A GLANCE AT Forster's life, with the hope of relating it to his work, presents the reader, at this late date, with a perplexing but pleasing paradox. Forster is a very old man. Born on January 1, 1879, he has witnessed as many major world events and cataclysms as most men now living can remember. He has also, after a certain point in his life—perhaps the age he had reached in the 1930's—begun to ally himself with the past. He has done so with unpretentiousness and with firmness, and he has never cast the future in the role of unmitigated villain. Yet the bonds between him and the past have increasingly strengthened. And here is the paradox. For those who enjoy his works, they not only remain relevant to our own day but show a remarkable resistance to fluctuations in taste. People still argue about *Howards End* and *A Passage to India*—which is the better of the two? But nobody denies that both belong to the permanent tradition of the English novel. And some would claim that all five of Forster's novels belong in that tradition. People still marvel that so delightful—and in many ways perfect—a novel as *Where Angels Fear to Tread* (1905) should have been published when Forster was only twenty-six; they marvel that so young a man should have launched his career as a novelist with so fine a book.

But, as Forster himself insists, it is one thing to talk about a man's books and another to talk about the man. Until recently, behind the disguise of ready and public utterance, Forster has remained elusive. A corollary is that the reader of the two biographies he has written— *Goldsworthy Lowes Dickenson* (1934) and *Marianne Thornton: A Domestic Biography: 1797–1887* (1956) — discovers that until very recently Forster has revealed more about himself when he has been writing about others than when he has been consciously assuming a public posture or making his opinion on a public issue the occasion for an essay or address. We turn to the two biographies to discover some of the most important thoughts and feelings that go into the making of Forster's own intellectual biography. But there have also been times when Forster has directly addressed the public; yet he has not assumed a public posture. His essays and talks, like the two biographies, are most valuable for an understanding of his own intellect and sensibility. Occasionally, they also relate to the themes of his stories and novels.

To speak of Forster's themes is to speak of his loves and beliefs. He has always made art out of the deepest currents of his affections and his awareness of his personal relation to tradition—Western, English, and familial. He is an artist because he has been able to school these affections and loyalties by his intellect. Personal relations—their possibilities and limitations, even their paradoxes—have concerned him throughout his life. In his art, "places"—a house, a familiar landscape, a city visited—have been caught up and held fast in the intricate web woven by his heart, mind, and eye. All the arts, but especially music, have both filled his private hours and supplied color and motifs to his writing. Hellenism, in its many manifestations, has often been a liberating influence upon his imagination. And then there is his loyalty to his own past, which usually comes to us indirectly through his art but which has also been made explicit in expository writing characteristized by the Forsterian manner and style, neither cheerful nor sad. In 1946 he wrote,

I belong to the fag-end of Victorian liberalism, and can look back to an age whose challenges were moderate in their tone, and the cloud on whose horizon was no bigger than a man's hand. In many ways it was an admirable age. It practised benevolence and philanthropy, was humane and intellectually curious. . . . The education I received in those far-off and fantastic days made me soft and I am very glad it did, for I have seen plenty of hardness since, and I know it does not even pay. . . . But . . . none of us realised our economic position. In came the nice fat dividends, up rose the lofty thoughts, and we did not realise that . . . we were exploiting the poor of our own country and the backward races abroad.[1]

Perhaps it is the tone of passages like the above—detached self-appraisal combined with frank attachment to values—that both disarms us and encourages us to make a place among modern voices for Forster's. E. H. Johnson has said that Forster's loyalty to his background and education has given him a "sense of the continuity of Europe's history and heritage . . . so that again and again his books give an impression of civilization."[2] Lionel Trilling has noted that the "great thing Forster has been able to learn from his attachment to tradition and from his sense of the past is his belief in the present."[3] More recently V. S. Pritchett has speculated that "Forster has survived so far by interposing. Where his elders, Shaw, Wells, Kipling imposed by sheer efficiency and manpower, Forster has interposed and influenced by . . . refusal to speak in a public voice. This has given the personal a startling strength."[4]

When all has been said, however, there is no final explanation of why a mind and personality rooted in tradition, especially in nineteenth-century English tradition, should continue to speak with strength to readers in the second half of the twentieth century. Perhaps an exhaustive explanation would have to focus as much on those of us who continue to gain pleasure from what Forster has written as it would on the man and his works. There is wisdom in John Beer's observation.

Nothing has yet taken the place of romanticism in the West. . . . Most modern attitudes are romantic attitudes.

But the fact that we describe them as "attitudes" betrays
the difference. The peculiar forces which drove romanticism
between the French Revolution and the First World War,
enabling it to inspire a whole way of life, have gone. They
will hardly combine again in a similar pattern.

To understand Forster fully, one has to see him at the
end of that earlier phase, the spiritual heir of Blake, Coleridge and Shelley, of Beethoven and Wagner. He shares
their aspirations and their struggles, while counterpoising
them with his grasp of human affairs.[5]

This is one possible historical approach to an understanding of Forster. A second, especially in an attempt to
construct his intellectual biography, is—as has been suggested—to search for revealing glimpses of the man in
what he has written about others.

Important to any understanding of Forster is his lineal
descent from the Evangelical Clapham Sect; his biography
of his great-aunt Marianne Thornton throws light on his
emotional, moral, and material connections with the
Evangelicals and their progeny. F. C. Crews reads in
Marianne Thornton an avowal by Forster that he regards
the Clapham Sect as his "intellectual starting-place," [6]
and although one suspects that Forster, *after* he had been
formed by later influences, accentuated—out of pride and
mature sympathy—his attachment to the Sect, his ties to
it are undeniable.

Forster's very act of writing *Marianne Thornton* is
suggestive and significant. At the outset Forster tells us,
"This biography is based almost entirely upon family papers. It is only concerned with them in their domestic
aspect, but scholars . . . who have looked at them report
that they are also interesting in other ways." [7] By "other
ways" Forster of course means nineteenth-century social,
political, and religious history; but his disarming modesty
is, in this instance, a good reason to focus on whatever
there is in the book that tells us something about E. M.
Forster and his origins, and to subordinate not only what
"scholars" have found in the family papers but the portrait of Marianne Thornton as well.

Of chief importance in the early pages of the book is Forster's description of Battersea Rise, the house of his Thornton ancestors, which fronted on the west side of Clapham Common. The historian will be interested to learn that William Wilberforce, the abolitionist, lived there for four years. The reader of Forster's novels and essays will note the authorial comment concerning Battersea Rise and the Thornton children. "It satisfied in them that longing for a particular place, a home, which is common amongst our upper and middle classes, and some of them transmitted that longing to their descendants, who have lived on into an age where it cannot be gratified (*MT, p. 5*). In many places and in many ways, we learn, as we read his other works, that Forster is one such descendant.

He is both proud of his Thornton ancestors and attached to many of their values. Although he calls these people "intellectual" rather than "artistic," he knows he is speaking of men and women who made nineteenth-century English history. He stresses their devotion to "good works" and refuses to share "the moral indignation" of people like the Hammonds, who perceive that the Clapham Sect helped to abolish slavery abroad but was blind to industrial slavery at home. Forster agrees with "the above line of criticism" but insists that "the really bad people . . . are those who do no good anywhere and help no one either at home or abroad" (*MT, p. 49*).

One gathers from this book evidence of Forster's fascination with trees, evidence ranging from the obvious effect upon his own imagination of Marianne Thornton's fear as a little girl that if Napoleon invaded England he would cut down the tulip tree upon the lawn of Battersea Rise to Forster's explicit statement, in the latter part of the book, that the wych-elm which stood near a house in which he and his mother once lived is the wych-elm in *Howards End.*

Of even broader interest is the Thornton connection with Cambridge. "Cambridge had been preferred to Oxford. It was supposed to be more in the Evangelical tradition: Wilberforce had been at John's . . . Henry Thornton and Tom Macaulay were entered together at Trinity" (*MT*, *p.* 77). Another fact learnt from *Marianne Thornton* tempts one to speculate also on the possibility of a connection between Forster and the Anglo-Irish tradition that has added so much color, vigor, and poetic grace to English literature in the last seventy-five years. His paternal grandfather, the Reverend Charles Forster, was Anglo-Irish, and "in the 'twenties he was eager and charming and a little foolish" (*MT*, *p.* 84). Forster's father, "Eddie," was one of ten children, and since the family was not well off, Marianne Thornton became their chief financial support, as well as Forster's grandmother's confidante (*MT*, *p.* 155).

Interesting is one of his references to Christmas tableaux, as they were presented at Battersea Rise. Although Forster never saw them in that house, he does "remember thinking them lovely half a century later, in my own childhood. What trouble must have been expended in draping and posing the loveliness! And how irrevocably it disappeared" (*MT*, *p.* 162). One thinks of his interest in the pageant-drama, of the many tableau-like scenes in his novels, and, most interestingly, of the expression in these scenes of some feeling or idea concerning the transitory and the permanent.

Cambridge occurs again when we are told that "there was a Forster-Thornton reunion at Cambridge—that academic stronghold of Evangelicism. It was the parliamentary election of July, 1847" (*MT.* *p.* 179).

"Domesticity" and "place," two important themes in much of his work, are obliquely illuminated in the account Forster gives of Henry Thornton's second marriage (to his deceased wife's sister—in defiance of the law of the day); and in Forster's account of the behavior of various individuals during the ensuing crises. One result of Henry's marriage was Marianne Thornton's removal from Battersea Rise, and it is clear that Forster's sympathetic understanding of her "domestic feelings" is deep. Forster records Marianne's description of her leave-taking from

Battersea Rise, ". . . it feels . . . a mixture of going to be married and going to die" (*MT, p. 201*). Referring to the wavering feelings of Henry Thornton's relatives, who had abandoned Battersea Rise after its owner's disturbing marriage, Forster says, "I understand many of their feelings: it has so happened that I have been deprived of a house myself. They will not be understood by the present generation" (*MT, p. 205*). Forster has probably alluded here to a painful period, the year 1946. "His mother had died, and his tenancy of the house in Abinger, Surrey, where they had lived together for many years was unexpectedly terminated by its owners." [8] If this is the episode in his own life to which Forster is referring, he has modestly underestimated the sympathetic understanding he can expect from readers of his work. He has immodestly underestimated the ability of such readers, even those who have never lived in a house like Battersea Rise or the one in Abinger, to imagine what the experience must be like.

Although in his own life the crisis of where to live next was resolved—Forster was offered permanent rooms in Kings College, Cambridge—the only Honorary Fellow ever to be so rescued from a personal dilemma—the story of Forster's lifelong attachment to his mother and to other women older than himself surely touches on the "domestic theme" in his work. It is that theme only which concerns us here. As for the biographical story, we can hope that it will someday be written by someone with the sense, imagination, and requisite taste to do so for a worthwhile purpose.[9]

There is enough in the Battersea Rise episode alone to enlarge our discussion of the "domestic theme" in Forster's work. Forster calls Marianne's departure from her brother's house a "disaster," and he devotes more pages to the event than he does to any death that occurs in the biography. Aware of the eighteenth- and nineteenth-century Puritan tendency to elaborate death and funerals—one-third of *Clarissa* is devoted to the preparation of the heroine for death and to the consequences of her dying—Forster, in the biography of his great aunt, as in his

novels, is determined to outwit this Puritanical predilec-
tion. In *Marianne Thornton* he not only does not quote
from papers that would evoke protracted death scenes but
tells us he has deliberately avoided doing so (he makes a
democratic exception in the case of the nurse—"Nurse
Hunter"—who attended the growing up of the Thornton
children). But crises surrounding houses, and to a lesser
extent neighborhoods, take the place of funereal drama,
sentiment, and ceremony.

We learn of the significance of Marianne Thornton in
Forster's father's life. "Eddie Forster, my father, became
Marianne's favourite nephew" (*MT, p. 234*). We learn
also that Forster's father went to Cambridge (Trinity)
and then became an architectural pupil in the office of Sir
Arthur Blomfield, where "there had previously been another pupil there: by name Thomas Hardy. It is one of
Life's Little Ironies that I should have got to know Mr.
Hardy and stayed with him at Max Gate, and should have
never known my father, seven years his junior" (*MT, p.
234*).

In the later pages of *Marianne Thornton*, Forster introduces himself. Informing us that one of Marianne's
friends was Julia Snow Wedgwood, Forster obligingly
adds, "Here we touch my own literary career, for I assisted
her in the revised edition of [*The Moral Ideal* (1907)].
She was an old lady then, and most pleasant to devil for"
(*MT, p. 247*). As for his grandmother (on his mother's
side), "How I adored my grandmother!—we played for
hours together. In later life I became high-minded and
critical, but we remained friends, and it is with her . . .
that my heart lies" (*MT, p. 279*).

We are given a fond description of Forster's mother,
Lily Wichelo (*MT, pp. 279–80*), and are told that Marianne was, surprisingly, delighted by the marriage of her
favorite nephew Eddie to a woman who was a governess at
the time. But unfortunately, Marianne had a tendency to
interfere, and in a few years Forster's mother was saying,
"Monie is a very wicked woman" (*MT, p. 282*).

But when Forster's father died, four years after marriage, E. M. Forster succeeded "as the favourite nephew" (*MT, p.* 289), and the feeling between Marianne and Lily Forster softened, a change which Forster is the first to admit has been important in his life. No doubt much can be made of his visits to the old lady in the last years of her life, to his mother's financial dependence upon her, but Forster's own conclusion to the biography of Marianne Thornton puts into the plainest—if still Forsterian— language her tangible influence upon his life. When she died, in 1887, she left E. M. Forster a legacy of £8,000.

> This £8,000 has been the financial salvation of my life. Thanks to it, I was able to go to Cambridge—impossible otherwise, for I failed to win scholarships. After Cambridge I was able to travel for a couple of years, and traveling inclined me to write. After my first visit to India and after the First World War the value of the £8,000 began to diminish, and later on it practically vanished. But by then my writings had begun to sell . . . . Whether—in so stormy an age as ours—this is a reputable sequence I do not know. . . . But I am thankful . . . to Marianne Thornton; for she . . . made my career as a writer possible, and her love, in a most tangible sense, followed me beyond the grave (*MT, pp.* 324–25).

We, too, are thankful to Marianne Thornton. Our thanks paid to her, we return to E. M. Forster, and to learn more about him as a youth, we apply to his biography of G. Lowes Dickenson.

From Dickenson's indictment of his own public school, Charterhouse, we get not only Forster's pungent comments on the English public school system but indirectly a view of his own experience at Tonbridge, his own school. "There is no reason to suppose that Charterhouse either was or is worse than our other leading educational hotels, but as generation after generation of sensitive boys record their experiences in them, one marvels why the boarding-house system continues at all, and why the middle classes still insist on so much discomfort for their children at such expense to themselves." [10]

When he discusses Dickenson's going up to King's Col-

lege, Cambridge, we learn what that experience meant to
Forster himself: "It seems too good to be real. That the
public school is not infinite and eternal, that there is
something more compelling in life than team-work and
more vital than cricket, that firmness, self-complacency
and fatuity do not between them compose the whole
armour of man, that lessons may have to do with leisure
and grammar with literature—it is difficult for an inexperi-
enced boy to grasp truths so revolutionary, or to realise
that freedom can sometimes be gained by walking out
through an open door." [11]

The reality of "freedom" and the "open door" are ques-
tionable today, but as a problem they are at least as
contemporary as the theme of Jean-Paul Sartre's *The
Flies*. More important, the two ideas have been actualities
in Forster's own career.

We learn something more of Forster as he continues to
discuss Dickenson's experience in college.

> As Cambridge filled up with friends it acquired a magic
> quality. Body and spirit, reason and emotion, work and
> play, architecture and scenery, laughter and seriousness, life
> and art—these pairs which are elsewhere contrasted were
> there fused into one. People and books reinforced one
> another, intelligence joined hands with affection, specula-
> tion became a passion, and discussion was made profound
> by love. When Goldie speaks of this magic fusion, he
> illumines more careers than his own, and he seems not only
> to epitomise Cambridge but to amplify it, and to make it
> the heritage of many who will never go there in the flesh. [12]

Matthew Arnold wanted Oxford to be the heritage, the
prevailing power, in the lives of many who would not go
there. Probably neither his wish nor Forster's assertion
about Dickenson has been borne out in the sense that
either was intended. But this much is fact: Forster, a
student in King's College, too, has written novels that are
the heritage of many of who have never been there and
may even know little or nothing about the school.

One of the chief characteristics of Forster's morality
and art is his constant guard against "muddle." At least

one critic has traced this spirit back to Cambridge, although not to the actual four years Forster spent there as an undergraduate. "A morality which lays so much stress on the importance of not getting muddled evidently owes something to the popularity of G. E. Moore's philosophy. *Principia Ethica* was published in 1903, two years after Forster graduated, and was widely discussed in Cambridge. Moore's chief point was that in our search for goodness we ought continually to be asking, 'What is a good state of mind?' And one very evident prerequisite of a good state of mind is that it should not be muddled." [13]

Excluding Forster's writing, the two main biographical facts of the years succeeding Cambridge are his travels and his association with the Bloomsbury group. Together, these considerations take us from the beginning of the twentieth century into the 1920's.

Forster's early travels, and their relationship to his work, have been competently summarized by H. J. Oliver.

> A first journey to Greece in 1901 (reflected in some of the short stories); a period at Alexandria during the 1914–18 war (leading to *Alexandria: A History and a Guide*, written in 1922 and revised in 1938, and *Pharos and Pharillon*, a 'collection of essays on Alexandrian themes' ancient and modern, in 1923); and at least three journeys to India (*A Passage to India* was drafted after the first of these in 1912–13 but completed after the second, of 1921; and *The Hill of Devi*, published in 1953, has given a full account of the second sojourn, when Forster was for six months Acting Private Secretary to the Maharajah of Dewas State Senior.) [14]

The third visit to India occurred in 1945 and is, for obvious historical reasons, of different significance in Forster's intellectual or artistic biography from the first two.

Forster's association with the Bloomsbury group brings us back to the influence of G. E. Moore's philosophy and also tells us who Forster's early friends were.

Commenting on Moore's influence on the Bloomsbury group, J. K. Johnstone has said that Moore's philosophy was cloistered but that members of the group, in practice if not in theory, were "creators or men and women of action" and thus acknowledged social and political realities as integral aspects of life not to be blinked away.[15] A logical addition here is Lionel Trilling's observation of Forster as a writer. Trilling speaks of Forster's "unremitting concern with moral realism" and adds, "All novelists deal with morality, but not all novelists, or even all good novelists, are concerned with moral realism, which is not the awareness of morality itself but of the contradictions, paradoxes, and dangers of living the moral life." [16]

It would be fruitless, in considering the truth of Trilling's observation, to try to decide how much of Forster's "moral realism" is owing to innate intelligence and imagination; how much to the years at Cambridge as an undergraduate; and how much to the influence of Moore's philosophy [17] and *its* influence upon the Bloomsbury group.

Nonetheless, in connection with the last named question, J. K. Johnstone is again interesting. He tells us that to the intrinsic goods enunciated in Moore's *Principia Ethica* — the love of beauty and the importance of personal relations — the Bloomsbury group added pursuit of knowledge.[18] Among the many ways in which Forster's works might be approached, one is surely legitimate: these works are a search for "knowledge" — of the escape from muddle, of the quest for moral realism, of a relation between life and artistic form in which the first is not weakened or made to play a perfunctory role.

Of interest to the biographical imagination — because the information invites speculation — are the people Forster met during the Bloomsbury period. These include Virginia and Leonard Woolf, the economist Lord Keynes, the influential art critics Clive Bell and Roger Fry, and the anti-Victorian dreadnought, Lytton Strachey.

Forster's early friendships and acquaintances take us also into the period of his emergence as a novelist — the years 1905 to 1910 — and it is the novels themselves that ought to be the focus of discussion of the period. By contrast, the years following A *Passage to India* (1924) reveal Forster as the writer of the public and private essay, and as a public speaker. Nonetheless, Forster's essays and talks after 1924 proceed with almost imperceptible continuity as responses to the First World War, the Depression, the rise of Fascism, the Second World War, and ultimately the postwar period and the present.

The closer we get to the present, the more clearly Forster is heard speaking openly and candidly about himself and his works—in published interviews and other printed matter. As for his public position, "[Forster] owes a good deal of his standing in the post-war world to the fact that he was not closely involved with any of the major political movements of the 'thirties. His individuality of position was due to a persistent awareness of the weakness of human nature, a tempering of his idealism by unwillingness to idealize human beings in the mass." [19] Further, "[Forster] accepts technological advances without sneering but also without enthusiasm. . . . In the mass-movements which technological organization encourages, Forster sees a menace to individuality and, to intelligence." [20]

Against the background of these large observations, the specific interviews that Forster in recent years has granted, as well as other more-or-less spontaneous and personal avowals, make sense.[21] In 1959 he told K. W. Gransden that "his order was the same as it always had been: first people, then books, then places." [22] In the same year, interviewed by David Jones, Forster informs us that his tutor, Nathaniel Wedd, suggested to him that he might be a writer. Forster muses about his reasons for ceasing to write novels after *A Passage to India*: "I somehow dried up after the *Passage*. I wanted to write but did not want to write novels. And that is really too long a story. But I think that one of the reasons why I stopped writing novels is that the social aspect of the world changed so much. I had been accustomed to write about the old-fashioned world with its homes and its family life and its comparative peace. All that went, and though I can think about the new world I cannot put it into fiction." [23]

Besides protesting that the story of why Forster stopped writing novels would not seem long at all, we notice that in giving "one reason" why he stopped writing novels, he catches up in a single sweep the years between 1924 and 1959, which to younger minds seem diverse and sharply divided into distinct periods.

In the interview Forster continues to speak of his own work. "I have only got down on to paper really three types of people: the person I think I am, the people who irritate me, and the people I would like to be." [24] He confirms the impressions we receive from his two collections of essays, *Abinger Harvest* (1936) and *Two Cheers for Democracy* (1951).

He informs us that he was influenced by Jane Austen,[25] Samuel Butler, and Proust, the last because "he has shown me a little what it is to be both delicate and deep as a novelist." [26] Forster says that Beethoven and Verdi are his favorite composers. As for Samuel Butler, he had earlier told Angus Wilson, "He taught me how to look at money when I was young." [27] We recall that Forster once planned to write a study of Butler and we reflect, in passing, that the role of money in *The Way of All Flesh* and in *Howards End* encourages an intriguing comparison and contrast. Further on occurs a reference to Virginia Woolf worth transcribing: "For me it's a matter of temperament. I stopped being influenced by Virginia when I knew that her feelings were not mine." [28]

In an interview granted to P. N. Furbank and F. J. H. Haskell, we learn that "in 1951 [Forster] produced a libretto for Benjamin Britten's opera *Billy Budd*." [29] We are told also that Forster once had an idea for an historical novel—with a Renaissance setting—but that nothing came of it.[30] There occurs at another point a familiar expression of the intellect, imagination, and temperament of the younger Forster. "I am more interested in achievement than in advance on it and decline from it. And I am more interested in works than in authors." [31] The man who on other occasions put people before books is not contradicting himself. He is telling us something about his aesthetic theory. In another assertion by Forster, his admirer will discover one of the grounds for pleasure in Forster's style, and the denigrator of Forster's work will also no doubt find support, "I have always found writing pleasant, and don't understand what people mean by 'throes of creation.' I've enjoyed it, but believe that in some ways it is good." [32]

Even a brief biographical outline ought to end by relating the past, the present, and the future of its subject. It should also, like all good stories, concern itself with good and evil. To fulfill these criteria in Forster's case, many ways will suggest themselves to the writer of a full biography. For our purposes, we will let Forster and two of his critics do the task in summary fashion.

In an essay on Forster's life, John Fuller indicts Forster's career and implicitly repudiates his work, "[Forster] has denied himself the ordinary experiences of life, of faith and the loss of faith; the dull turbulence of family life, the stretching of one's full powers, as a soldier, or a scientist, or in the corrupt and confusing area of activity which any large civilian organization presents to those who would push humanity forward a little, in its strange and uncertain venture, towards a comely and desirable life." [33]

One of Forster's own statements about the future is an unintentional defense against Fuller. "The only way science can help us in the future is psychologically. Not physically. It has gone far too far in the physical direction. It is the old phrase—we must have a change of heart. And I think that cannot be expressed in scientific terms, and that it is by altering ourselves and helping others to alter that we may get through the frightful crisis that has been induced by our own ingenuity." [34] In juxtaposition to Fuller's words, Forster's are apposite if for no other reason than that Forster's approving reference to science is an approval of action.

The concluding observation about the meaning of Forster's past and present, his implications for the future, the play in his career of negation and affirmation—good and evil—is V. S. Pritchett's. "It is easy enough to demonstrate that Forster represents the end of something. He has almost said so himself, though not quite: civilisations are a string of intermissions in the anger of time. He speaks at the end of liberal culture and, since there is no other, there is no implicit accusation. He agrees that this firm attachment owes something to privilege and we all know the dogma that, in its penultimate phase, a culture sees spiritual order in art alone; in its ultimate post-Forsterian phase it crumbles into a sort of Byzantine pedantry." [35]

For anyone who shares Pritchett's view of the present, turning at this point to Forster's stories and novels will be going not back but forward.

2   SHORT STORIES AND ARCTIC SUMMER

IN AN INTRODUCTION written in 1947 for a collected edition of his short stories, Forster says that "these fantasies were written at various dates previous to the first world war."[1] Like his early travels, the stories follow Cambridge in his career, and the shaping influence of his college experience is the first element in the tales to consider. Of prime importance is the felt knowledge of Greek mythology, acquired by Forster as an undergraduate, made vivid by his travels. Worth noting, too, is that Dickenson's *The Greek View of Life* (1896), "a lucid summary of the Hellenism . . . popular at the time," had strongly appealed to Forster, "and both the quality and the force of its enthusiasm for Greece carry over into Forster's books."[2]

Dickenson's influence provides another way of looking at Forster's short stories. It invites us to expect paradox and polarity in them. Despite Forster's description of the tales as "fantasies" only, realism often subtly opposes fantasy. In a few of the *Collected Short Stories*, it even dominates fantasy. Dickenson's Hellenism vied with his conviction that he had discovered in the Greece of antiquity a form of reality applicable to his own times, and many of his activities seem an attempt to demonstrate, or apply to the public world, his beliefs. He was one of the founders, in 1903, of the monthly *Independent Review*.[3] Forster has written that "It was not so much a Liberal review as an appeal to Liberalism from the Left to be its better self." He continues.

"The Independent Review" did not make much difference to the councils of the nation, but it struck a note which was new at that time, and had great influence on a number of individuals. . . . Those who were Liberals felt that the heavy, stocky, body of their party was about to grow wings. . . . Those who were not Liberals were equally filled with hope: they saw avenues opening into literature, philosophy, human relationships, and the road of the future passing through not insurmountable dangers to a possible Utopia.[4]

These words would be apposite here if for no other reason than that Forster dedicated the first volume of his short stories to *The Independent Review*. "This was a monthly," Forster wrote in 1947, in the introduction to his *Collected Short Stories*, "controlled by an editorial board of friends who had encouraged me to start writing" (*p. 6*).

The period when his short stories were written is therefore one in which Forster was intimately associated with a nonmaterialistic radicalism in political and social thinking, a radicalism which, however sophisticated and spiritualized, led to a preoccupation with class. "Class" can, in fact, be seen in the short stories as the polar opposite of "fantasy." The continuous play of class realism against fantasy leads to both the successes and failures of the short stories.

Italian waiters, fishermen, porters; Greek peasants and keepers of dirty, impoverished countryside inns all appear in Forster's short stories. They have less money than do the English tourists whose lives become fatefully linked with their own. Because the Greeks and Italians are always inferior in social station to the English tourists, class and nationality become interchangeable.

These facts are evident in "The Story of a Panic"—the first tale Forster ever wrote (*p. 5*), "The Road from Colonus," "The Story of the Siren," and "The Eternal Moment." In other stories, class values and conflicts *within* England are the themes. If we enlarge our own vision to embrace simultaneously the two poles—class realism and the antithetical fantasy upon which the tales are richly woven or thinly stretched—a significant aspect of the stories is revealed. It is one, interestingly, that is not always consistent with ideas expressed in Forster's novels of the same period, particularly in A *Room with a View.*

Though committed, in the tales, to progressive, ameliorative social thinking, Forster could not see the future illuminated—clear and detailed—in the light of a new dawn.[5] Humane, but also rational and skeptical, he colors his short stories with a suggestion that only for the naïve is the future a real country. The alternative to social injustice or constriction is not revolution, or even a prophetic vision. It is an escape into the woods that have been deserted by conventional middle-class Englishmen.

To make the escape effective, Forster endows with magical powers those who are in flight; or else he exposes them to special experiences unavailable to the class bound. These powers or experiences bring about the fulfillment of the escapees and become the measure of their superior strength, as well as the beginning, for them, of a new life. An alternative to Trilling's judgment that "the Greek myths made too deep an impression on Forster"[6] therefore suggests itself. Given Forster's political skepticism, the Greek myths congenially substitute moral-poetic statement for action—in the struggle to escape the immoral, life-denying constraints of middle-class life.

Some may argue that the use of magic to defeat the repressions of society is childlike, but to do so is to ignore Forster's skill as an artist. Through every device—mood, tone, characterization, relations of characters to each other and to society—he convinces us that realistic escape is impossible. Magic therefore becomes, in the stories, not a child's means of creating pretended power, but a poetic device on Forster's part for expressing his compassion for suffering characters and his conviction that something noble and valuable in them is being wasted before they escape. Insofar as he makes us feel the compassion, too, makes us share the sense of loss—and relief when the wasting of life ends—he succeeds.

"The Story of a Panic," first in the *Collected Short Stories,* compels interest. Its central character is Eustace

Robinson, a fourteen-year-old spoiled, lethargic English boy who is accompanying a party of English adults, on tour and staying near Ravello. The narrator obligingly establishes himself as all that is obnoxious in middle-class Englishmen. For the wrong reasons, he objects to Eustace's apathy, "I would not have minded so much if he had been a really studious boy, but he neither played hard nor worked hard" (p. 10). As an inkling of England's future, Eustace does not promise much; but Mr. Tytler (the narrator), as a representative of England's present—at the beginning of the century—is equally bleak.

Annoyed at Eustace, the narrator declares that the boy is in need of "discipline." As a virtue, "discipline" is Apollonian. As a mark of class, it connotes, at the beginning of the century, those who govern. But in the absence of any other social and personal values of any worth, it is an empty and useless form—worse than useless, for it does succeed in killing off any impulse on the part of the individual to come alive. But there is hope—magical, mythical hope: to be touched by Pan, the Dionysian spirit, and consequently to become related again to all of nature.

On a picnic attended by a touring party, Pan suddenly makes his presence felt. All, except Eustace, panic and flee. Mr. Tytler, describing the episode, confesses the sexual fears—the snobbery concerning sex—of himself and his class, "And it was no ordinary humiliation that survived; for I had been afraid, not as a man, but as a beast" (p. 15). Pan cannot heal him. The Dionysian experience is reserved for the poor, and for a fourteen-year-old boy. Eustace, alone on the picnic site, is touched by Pan, sleeps, and awakens to a new life. But Eustace is a child, and as such he is, for the middle classes, a poetic symbol of hope, not a socially or politically viable image of a better future.

As the English party makes its way back to the hotel, Eustace, whose energetic antics have been amazing everybody, kisses the cheek of an old woman who has been gathering fuel in the woods. Pan, the Dionysian spirit, is also the spirit of democracy. Back at the hotel, only Gennaro, an illiterate servant, understands what has happened to Eustace. He can understand because his social position has saved him from spiritual death.

The social issue, colored in this story by nationalism, is made explicit. Mr. Tytler hears Gennaro address Eustace with "Tu," and reprimands the Italian, "You are not right. You must use 'Lei' or 'Voi' — more polite forms. And remember that, though Signor Eustace is sometimes silly and foolish . . . you must always behave respectfully to him; for he is a young English gentleman, and you are a poor Italian fisher boy" (*p.* 23).

But Forster no sooner makes explicit the link between democracy and the spirit of life than his own spirit of political skepticism in such matters begins to preside. Mr. Tytler knows that "An honest English fisherman would have landed me one in the eye in a minute for such a remark" (*p.* 23) and *we* no longer know just what the link between democracy and magic is supposed to be, since presumably in England there can be democracy without magic. Moreover, Gennaro becomes somewhat more complex, and his complexity is mixed up with a reestablishment of class difference and nationalism. He betrays Eustace into captivity for money, then enables him to escape from confinement in a hotel room — one "without a view" — that would have meant death for the boy. But it is Gennaro, clutching the money, who dies in the jump from the window.

Did he hope to have it both ways — to free Eustace for a nocturnal lifesaving romp in the woods and at the same time to cheat the enemy — Mr. Tytler — out of his own magical power, money? Does Gennaro die because he once betrayed Eustace? It hardly seems likely, since Eustace not only escapes that night but lives to become some sort of vaguely hinted at social success. It seems more likely that Gennaro's death symbolizes the incompatibility of his desires: money, and service in behalf of life. Anyone, of any class or nationality, might be the victim of such contradictory desires. Yet in this story Forster seems to be saying that Gennaro must die because in taking money he has somehow sacrificed the simplicity and purity of life that is the portion of a poor Italian fisherboy.

The social implications are thus somewhat obscured rather than clarified by the clash of two very different kinds of magic: the power of Pan to cleanse and rejuvenate and the power of money to corrupt and kill. The story *does* have it both ways: Eustace lives and prospers; Gennaro dies, because "Something had gone wrong inside him" (*p.* 33).

At the conclusion we are left with a set of uncomfortable metaphysical problems. Why are there two, historically incompatible, forms of magical power in the story? Why does the older one—Pan—save Eustace for a thriving life in a society based upon money? Why does the new one—money—have the power to kill Gennaro even though he has not foresworn allegiance to Pan? Why, in other words, can Pan protect middle-class Eustace, for a life time, against the corrupting power of money; but cannot or will not protect Gennaro? The answer to these metaphysical questions, if there is one, must be drawn from an unmetaphysical source. Forster's deep-down conviction is that the spiritually dead but educated middle class can more easily undergo transformation, become vital again, than the peasantry representing the simplicity of the past, can resist the former's corrupting influence.

The answer suggested above also illuminates "The Eternal Moment," first published in 1905.[7] Significantly, "The Eternal Moment" is one of the two published short stories by Forster not dependent on fantasy. Without denigrating spiritual values, Forster, in "The Eternal Moment," squarely faces the intractability of realistic class conditions and processes.

Twenty years before the time of the story, Miss Raby, a successful English novelist, had visited the town of Vorta, in Italy. On a mountain trip, a young porter, Feo Ginori, had surprised her by passionately addressing words of love to her. Even though his "oration" had been "prepared out of *I Promessi Sposi*" (*p.* 189), the handsome peasant simplicity and the ardor of the man had combined with the extraordinary details of the situation to turn the event, for Miss Raby, into "The Eternal Moment," the title she gave to the novel based upon Feo and his suit to her.

As a result of the novel, Miss Raby and the town of Vorta were launched—Miss Raby on a career as a writer; the town as a tourist center. But the village, important in Miss Raby's novel because it had something to offer the middle-class world, has been corrupted.

> A village must have some trade; and this village had always been full of virility and power. . . . Civilization did not relax these energies, but it had diverted them; and all the precious qualities, which might have helped to heal the world, had been destroyed. . . . No villain had done this thing: it was the work of ladies and gentlemen who were good and rich and often clever—who, if they thought about the matter at all, thought that they were conferring a benefit, moral as well as commercial, on any place in which they chose to stop (*p. 205*).

Feo has also changed. He is now the multilingual concierge of the newest and most expensive hotel in the region. He has changed because "Intercourse with the gentle classes had required new qualities—civility, omniscience, imperturbality. It was the old answer: the gentle classes were responsible for him. . . . It was absurd to blame Feo for his worldliness—for his essential vulgarity" (*p. 212*).

After twenty years, Miss Raby revisits Vorta with Colonel Leyland, whom she is considering as a husband. She is convinced, when she arrives, that the past moment of spiritual joy and fulfillment is eternal. She reminds Feo of the long-ago incident, only to be greeted first by a blank memory, then by consternation, and finally by a vulgar wink. At the last, she rebukes Feo and passes to a new stage of understanding.

> For she realized that only now was she not in love with him: that the incident upon the mountain had been one of the great moments of her life . . . certainly the most enduring: that she had drawn unacknowledged power and inspiration from it . . . . There was more reality in it than

in all the years of success . . . which had followed . . . .
For all her correct behaviour and lady-like display, she had
been in love with Feo, and she had never loved so greatly
again (*pp.* 216–17).

Here, then, is one theme of the story. Feo, like Gennaro
in "The Story of a Panic," has saved a member of the
English middle class from a life of spiritual sterility. But
Feo's utter corruption is more realistic and threatening
than Gennaro's death. Feo's youthful simplicity and ardor
were drawn from the values of the village, rather than
from any internal moral strength or imaginative sensibility: as the village goes bad, so necessarily must Feo.

However, the question of class and nationality is, in this
story, more subtly yet clearly controlled than it was in
"The Story of a Panic." Miss Raby's voluble confrontation of the perplexed Feo, before the guests at the Hotel
des Grand Alpes, not only starts a ripple of tittering gossip
but alienates Colonel Leyland. The very end of the story
emphasizes class. When Miss Raby realizes that she is
truly alone in her understanding, and abruptly leaves the
two men, nobody calls after her. "Colonel Leyland would
have liked to do so; for he knew she must be unhappy. But
she had hurt him too much; she had exposed her thoughts
and desires to a man of another class. Not only she, but he
himself and all their equals, were degraded by it. She had
discovered their nakedness to the alien" (*p.* 221).

As a conclusion, Colonel Leyland's thoughts are effective, drawing their strength not only from the class analysis they create but from the link between Colonel Leyland
and Feo. A moment earlier we had been told that Miss
Raby had no pity for Colonel Leyland as he revealed
himself embarrassed by her forthrightness toward Feo.
Colonel Leyland had been well born and had had all the
"things called advantages, . . . And he had proved himself
to be at the exact spiritual level of the man who had no
advantages, who was poor and had been made vulgar,
whose early virtue had been destroyed by circumstance,
whose manliness and simplicity had perished in serving
the rich" (*pp.* 220–21).

The link is reinforced by the final words of the story. By dinner time, Colonel Leyland has forgotten his aborted desire to help Miss Raby in her unhappiness. All his efforts are now bent on diminishing the "scandal"; his crude plan is to reach an understanding with Feo that Miss Raby had been out of her mind. "Much as Colonel Leyland disliked touching people he took Feo by the arm, and then quickly raised his finger to his forehead. 'Exactly, sir,' whispered the concierge. 'Of course we understand—Oh, thank you, sir, thank you very much: thank you very much indeed!' " (*p. 222*).

In bribing his brother-under-the-skin, who squeals with delight—not at the acknowledgment of brotherhood but at the munificence of the bribe—Colonel Leyland not only makes more credible all the apparent themes of the story—class snobbery; the power of class and money to corrupt; the unromantic and essentially democratic reasons for the virtue of Vorta twenty years previously. He also unintentionally lends weight and approval to Miss Raby's valid romanticism. Although both the Colonel and Feo are unattractive, only the former is really guilty. Forster seems to be saying that the advantages of superior class and education are true values but impose a responsibility: to free for development the inadequate heart that has so far been one of their characteristics.

It is not *noblesse oblige* that Forster has in mind. He is quite unsentimental and realistic about the power for evil that the corrupted poor actually have. His concern with class has an artistic and spiritual aim rather than a political one. The irony and political skepticism implicit in the brotherhood of Colonel Leyland and Feo are public issues; but Colonel Leyland's ultimate guilt is private, not public. It is not that he has corrupted the already corrupted—and corruption prone—Feo. It is that despite all his advantages Colonel Leyland could fashion only an insensitive self that takes corruption for granted. In this story, morality and psychology combine with class to form a single polar opposite to fantasy.

Two of the best stories are "Other Kingdom" and "The

Road from Colonus," both included in Forster's earliest collection of tales, *The Celestial Omnibus* (1911). The first is a fantasy dependent on myth, the second is realistic. Each, in its own genre, is preeminently successful.

At the outset of "Other Kingdom," a classics lesson is taking place on the estate of the Worters family. Evelyn Beaumont, who is the fiancée of Harcourt Worters, reads from her notebook: "Gods. Where. . . . Pan—most places, as name implies. . . . Dryads—trees" (*p.* 59). Not only has a realistic event been described, but fantasy has, for the moment, been relegated to books and lessons.

The story turns on a reversal of this subordination, for at the end Evelyn has become a dryad to escape marriage with Harcourt, a humorless, strong-willed, unimaginative tyrant. Harcourt, as a lover, is reminiscent of two characters Forster developed in his novels: Cecil Vyse of *A Room with a View* (1908), and Henry Wilcox of *Howards End* (1910). Harcourt's lovemaking is also strikingly similar to Meredith's Sir Willoughby Patterne's, "[Harcourt] took out his pen-knife and drew [Evelyn] away in search of an unsullied tree. 'E. B., Eternal Blessing. Mine! Mine! . . .' " (*p.* 74). Up to a point, Evelyn's behavior resembles that of Clara Middleton, the "natural" girl in Meredith's *The Egoist* who is to marry Sir Willoughby. Jack Ford, Evelyn's classics teacher, bears a rough resemblance to another character in *The Egoist*, Vernon Whitford, whom Clara does marry.

Ultimately, however, through subordinate realism and predominant fantasy, Forster moves into territory unexplored by Meredith. Money kills—physically or spiritually —as we saw it kill Gennaro, Feo, and Colonel Leyland. It has contributed to the spiritual death of Harcourt Worters, and its pervasive power is made explicit when Jack Ford says to Evelyn, "Oh, there's no dodging Midas! He just comes, he touches you, and you pay him several thousand percent at once" (*p.* 60).

Midas has touched Harcourt Worters, and part of the strength of the story is the fact that in paying his "several thousand percent" Harcourt not only lives with an unde-

veloped heart but injures others. He makes Evelyn give up
her lessons in Latin and Greek. He no sooner presents her
with Other Kingdom, a copse adjoining his estate, than he
begins to think about "improvements": a fence to keep
the villagers out, a bridge across the stream that separates
his land from Other Kingdom, and an asphalt path from
his house into this wooded sanctuary that was to belong to
Evelyn.

His insensitive use of the power of money begins to
distress and frighten her. But the last blow is Harcourt's
dismissal of Jack Ford, who has written, in a private
notebook, amatory verses addressed to Evelyn. She cries
out to Mr. Inskip, the narrator, "I've failed with Harcourt.
. . . He won't let me do what I want. Latin and Greek
began it: I wanted to know about gods and heroes and he
wouldn't let me: then I wanted no fence round Other
Kingdom and no bridge and no path—and look! Now I
ask that Mr. Ford, who has done nothing, shan't be punished for it—and he is to go away for ever" (*p.* 79).

This is the turning point, and it requires Forster's complete skill. Mr. Inskip explains to Evelyn that Jack is being
punished for impertinence. " 'Impertinence is nothing!'
she cried. 'It doesn't exist. It's a sham, like "claims" and
"position" and "rights." It's part of the great dream' " (*p.*
79). Evelyn has spoken rhetorically, possibly metaphysically but, with a surer instinct than he displayed in "The
Story of a Panic," Forster makes us believe that the class-
conditioned "dream" comprising Harcourt's world is not
more real than is a Greek myth. Unable to live in Harcourt's dream world, Evelyn escapes into her own, one in
which "claims," "position," and "rights" are convincingly
unreal. She becomes a dryad, a spirit dwelling in Other
Kingdom.

Delicately balancing class and myth, Forster sends Harcourt, whose impoverished imagination can conceive only
that Evelyn has run off to Jack Ford, charging down upon
the latter. Jack is discovered living with his aunt, "in a
squalid suburb" of London. Part of the percentage that
the touch of Midas upon Harcourt has exacted has been

the economic ruin of Jack. But Jack's mind is a country of its own, a psychological equivalent of Evelyn's escape. When Harcourt demands to know where Evelyn is, Jack says, "I could tell you if I chose, but it would be no good, for she has not practically escaped you. She has escaped you absolutely, for ever and ever, as long as there are branches to shade men from the sun" (*p. 85*).

There are no contradictions among the connotations of this conclusion. Regarded as a poetic statement that a loving spirit can, in a world of squalor produced by the unequal consequences of the touch of Midas, shelter a sensitive spirit, the story is as relative to "reality" (if reality be equated with what men experience in life) as would be a story that dealt simply and literally with the passion of jealousy and the fact of social injustice.

Most critics agree that one of the best of Forster's short stories is "The Road from Colonus." It is an inverted equivalent of "Other Kingdom." Just as realism is successfully subordinated to fantasy and myth in "Other Kingdom"—subordinated but not erased—so in "The Road from Colonus" mystery is subordinated to realism yet remains at the conclusion as a felt presence.

Mr. Lucas, an aged Englishman, stops at a village near Colonus. Accompanying him on his tour of Greece are his daughter Ethel, who in the sequence reveals herself to be "a false Antigone";[8] a young man named Graham; and a Mrs. Forman, presumably a chaperone for Ethel. Mr. Lucas decides to stay awhile in Greece. But his reasons are ambiguous. Just prior to seeing water pour from a hollow tree, as Moses saw water come from the rock, Mr. Lucas says, "Greece is the land for young people . . . but I will enter into it, I will possess it. Leaves shall be green again, water shall be sweet, the sky shall be blue. . . . I do mind being old, and I will pretend no longer" (*p. 97*). Reading these lines, we seem to hear the protest of W. B. Yeats or Dylan Thomas against old age. But as the story develops, we see that the relief for old age really sought by Mr. Lucas is death.

Although Mr. Lucas wants to stay in Greece, he is

forced by his daughter and Graham to return to England. Some time later, unwrapping a present from Greece done up in old newspaper, Ethel reads that a tree—presumably the hollow tree from which the water of life had gushed—had blown down in the night and crushed the inhabitants of the little inn nearby. The place and date indicate that the accident occurred at the very place and time Mr. Lucas had wanted to stay. The peasants killed had been eager for Mr. Lucas to remain, and he had felt affinity with them. Ethel tells her father what had happened and reminds him how close he came to being killed: that he would have been killed had she and Mr. Graham not thwarted his will.

For Mr. Lucas, life has been reduced to grumbling about the chatter of the children next door, the barking of a dog, and the sound of running water—in pipes, not a hollow tree. His answer to his daughter's breathless speech is that he must write to the landlord, announcing that because of these noises he is giving up the house.

The point is clear; the story powerfully done, despite the somewhat obvious symbolism of the conclusion. The power is there because Forster is on sure ground. In this story, the English middle class of the early twentieth century is not only ignorant of how to live but of how to die. Just as it represses the life impulse in the young, it thwarts the desire of an old man who, having risen above the common outlook, wants to choose the time, place, and manner of his own death.

Mr. Lucas is not Achilles. He is not, despite the obvious associations, a convincing Oedipus. He is as much the Moses who has seen the water gush miraculously from the rock but does not live to see the promised land as he is, allegorically, a Greek. Nevertheless, his death in the home-land of Western glory, among members of the only modern class that still accepts death—the peasantry—would have been timely, noble, and fitting. The pitiful, meaningless fretting out in England of his useless days, for which he has been forcibly saved, is ignoble.

Like "Other Kingdom," "The Road from Colonus"

succeeds in part because it does not beg political or social questions. It makes personal relations, including one's relation to oneself, the central and excluding focus of our feelings and our interest. Although class is employed — Ethel's middle-class snobbery and ignorance of self-respect versus the Greek peasants' closeness to both instinctual life and literal death — Mr. Lucas's problem is not one that is likely to be solved by reconstructing political and social institutions. The successful paradox is that the idea of the story, precisely because it is properly limited, is too large to be encompassed by political and social theory. Theorists have not yet told us how to bring back the green leaves and blue skies of youth. Since these are what Mr. Lucas wants, death is, for him, a rational choice. The story is powerful because it is consistent and self-sufficient.

Although the four stories discussed so far seem to me to be Forster's best, the other eight in *Collected Short Stories*, as well as the unincluded tale, "Albergo Empedocle," and the fragment of a novel begun before World War I, but never finished, are not without interest.

"The Celestial Omnibus" is a fantasy through which Forster airs his early views on the value of great literature and its place in the over-all scheme of social and personal interests. A small boy and a pompous adult ride in the company of the immortals of literature. Mr. Bons, the "cultivated" gentleman of the middle classes, finds that, cut off from his moorings in conventional surroundings, he does not have the spiritual courage to become intimate with literature, and he falls from the fantasy heaven to death on the streets of London. For Forster, the cultural impostor deserves a worse fate than does the out-and-out philistine.

"The Machine Stops" is, Forster tells us (*p.* 6), a critique of H. G. Wells' faith in scientific progress. In Forster's science-fiction fantasy about the future, in which man for a time lives completely underground and transforms himself from master of the machine into its idolator, the talk of Kuno, the rebel-hero, about the stars is reminiscent of Blake. Incorporating a humanistic tradition

that began before Blake and still has adherents today, are
Kuno's words to Vashti, his mother, when she visits him,
"Man is the measure. That was my first lesson. Man's
feet are the measure for distance, his hands are the measure for ownership, his body is the measure for all that is
lovable and desirable and strong" (*p. 125*). Forster also
takes occasion to use George Meredith as a whipping boy.
Just before the machine stops, an unattractive lecturer
quotes Meredith's poetry to describe the ultimate goal of
the underground, scientific civilization as a generation
"seraphically free/From taint of personality" (*p. 136*).

The story ends ambivalently, on a note somewhere between pessimistic irony and optimism about man's ability
to learn from his mistakes. Here we get an inkling of
Forster's strengths and weaknesses in the tales. His optimism is most convincing when it is associated with personal relations; it is least convincing when it is made to
puff the sails of some prophetic or merely public declara-
tion about society conceived as an abstraction. Conversely,
his pessimism seems most natural, as we have seen in
"The Eternal Moment," when it is based on a view of
social processes.

A slight story like "The Other Side of the Hedge" gains
poignancy from social pessimism. The poignancy is effective because the narrator of "The Other Side of the
Hedge" not only dislikes the social processes already producing in 1904 the machine-worshipping civilization of
"The Machine Stops" but knows that he cannot oppose
these processes; he can only recognize the evils they pro-
duce and the brutality to which they subject the non-
aggressive members of society.

Thus, in this fantasy the narrator does accurately describe feeling and action in an industrialized world. He
says that "it was only the monotony of the highway that
oppressed me" (*p. 34*). Forster is accurately prophetic.
The subsequent years of the twentieth century have disclosed a succession of ills caused by monotony.

Another statement made by the narrator, although
somewhat ambiguous, has also become even more relevant

than it was when Forster wrote the story. "And I had already dropped several things—indeed the road behind was strewn with the things we all had dropped"; moreover, he continues, "My muscles were so weary that I could not even bear the weight of those things I still carried" (*p. 34*). Whether he has had to drop part of his more valuable cultural heritage, along with what W. H. Auden has called the "heterogeneous dreck" of our civilization, is not clear. The tone of the story is melancholy enough to suggest a negation of some kinds of art as well as of useless information and gadgets.

But what is of value is explicit. On "the other side of the hedge" the narrator sees a young man racing— alone—and hears a girl singing, though she has no audience but herself. Thus he learns what ought to be the rule on our side of the hedge: whatever is done should mean nothing but itself. And if the lesson seems too esoteric or decadent, Forster, at the end of the story, reminds us that the ultimate destiny of "our race"—an aggregate of individuals not an abstraction—is death.

As for the story called "The Point of It," in recent years he has been so modestly helpful that he has endangered our understanding of the tale. In the preface he wrote in 1947 for his *Collected Short Stories*, Forster says, "It was ill-liked when it came out by my Bloomsbury friends. 'What *is* the point of it?' they queried thinly, nor did I know how to reply" (*p. 6*). But the point of the story, however obscure or complex it may ultimately be, surely contains some veiled criticism of Bloomsbury behavior and attitudes, if not of the group's more fundamental theories and values.

The story is about two men, Micky and Harold, who are first seen in their youth. Harold dies by overexerting himself while rowing, and Micky asks, "What is the point of it?" Years later, Micky also dies; after a safe, sane, trivial, and wasted life. He produced nothing of importance except a son, Adam, who sees the emptiness of his father's life.

Micky awakens from death in a dusty, sandy infinity reminiscent of Dante's hell. He is suffering for having

committed the worst sins that unsympathetic critics had
alleged against the Bloomsbury group, and that Bloomsbury had alleged against the Victorians. He is "suffering
for all the praise that he had given to the bad and medio-
cre upon earth . . . for all the praise that had not been
winged with passion" (*p.* 159). The point, then, is that
Achilles made the right choice; as did Tennyson's Ulysses;
as did, finally, the young man Harold of Micky's youth,
who had not lost "the keen, heroic edge" and therefore
gave his life in a "pointless" battle against the sea.

"The Story of the Siren," thought by some to be one of
Forster's better short stories, is ultimately unsatisfying
because its theme is too big for its compass. The opening
lines, spoken by the narrator—a young Englishman writing a dissertation on the Deist controversy and, like other
characters in Forster's short stories, a member of a tourist
party in Italy—indicate that the story will deal with the
controversy between the expectation of the rational mind
and the experience of the total human being. "Few things
have been more beautiful than my note-book on the Deist
Controversy as it fell downward through the waters of the
Mediterranean" (*p.* 179). The juxtaposition of the abstract Nordic mind and the concrete, sensual Mediterranean world implicit in this description, plus the word
"beautiful," which in context suggests something more
than irony, is suggestive of both Albert Camus' and Thomas Mann's preoccupation with the difference between
the Nordic and Mediterranean worlds, different as their
ideas ultimately are from each other's and from Forster's.

The story is about a Sicilian man and wife who have
seen the Siren, a symbol, in Forster's work, of good-
and-evil. The wife, pregnant, is drowned by a priest; and
the man, Giuseppe, dies searching for someone else who
has seen the Siren. Giuseppe has loved and has been
loved, "but that is a different thing from being good" (*p.*
182). Giuseppe is, in fact, cruel and slothful. But the
point is that he is capable of both love and cruelty. Moreover, love, in the real world, is no guarantee of happiness, because the real world has not yet been "saved."

In the present world, the story seems to say, love can exist only in a context of cruelty and unhappiness. However, the alternative to love is silence and loneliness. The Saviour, who will be a composite of the mortal and divine, somewhat like W. B. Yeats's cyclical Saviour, will equate love with song. He will make it possible, in choosing love, rather than silence and loneliness, to experience love as happiness, not cruelty and sorrow.

The theme is, indeed, a large one, and although Forster concludes the story rather weakly—by having the other members of the tourist party return and thus prevent the student from asking the Sicilian narrator more, it is perhaps just as well that the discussion—and the story—is brought to an end at this point. A proper exploration of the theme would require either the true brevity of a great poem or the reasonable length of a fair-sized novel.

The first story Forster ever published, "Albergo Empedocle," was not included in either of the two volumes he subsequently put together or in the *Collected Short Stories* of 1947. Whatever the reason for its neglect by Forster, it deserves attention here. Although not one of Forster's best, it is interesting in theme and technique. It is a fantasy but it is also a morality tale concerning the fate of imagination in the modern world. Once again we are given a party of English tourists: Sir Edwin and Lady Peaslake; their daughter Mildred; a sister who plays a minor role; and Harold, Mildred's fiancé.

At the beginning of the story Mildred is presumably Harold's intellectual superior, " 'It is the imagination,' she would say, 'that makes the past live again,' " to which, " 'Rather!' was the invariable reply of Harold, who was notoriously deficient in it. . . . He was fairly rich, fairly healthy, very much in love, very fond of life, and he was content to worship in Mildred those higher qualities which he did not possess himself." [9] Sir Edwin unknowingly sets the facts in proper order.

Mildred he could pardon. . . . Besides, he shrewdly guessed that, although she might sometimes indulge in fancies, yet when it came to action she could be trusted to behave in a thoroughly conventional manner. . . . she was seldom guilty of confusing books with life.

But Harold did not escape so easily, for Sir Edwin absolutely failed to understand him . . . . Harold's character . . . consisted of little more than two things, the power to love and the desire for truth, and Sir Edwin, like many a wise thinker, concluded that what was not complicated could not be mysterious.[10]

Harold falls into a deep sleep on the rocks near the sea. He awakens to the realization that he has lived before, that he was Empedocles. At first Mildred is enchanted by this unwonted display of imagination in Harold, and not only says that she believes him but temporarily convinces herself that she, too, lived before—and loved Harold as Empedocles. But Harold, for whom the reincarnation is the real thing, comes to realize that Mildred has only been playing at the matter, and Mildred herself gradually realizes that she was self-deceived. This realization is too much for her. She is distressed by the thought that Harold might regard her as a hypocrite; yet she cannot conceive asking forgiveness "for to her forgiveness meant the triumph of one person over another." [11]

Deficient in character and imagination, Mildred repudiates her belief that Harold is Empedocles. When she withdraws her support, Harold suffers a breakdown and is confined to an institution in England, where he speaks a strange language which experts say is not Greek but which the narrator, Harold's former college roommate, suggests might be Greek spoken in a manner lost to the modern ear.

Soon everyone except the narrator forgets and neglects Harold. The narrator recognizes the value to Harold of male loyalty, but grasping the threads of both fantasy and psychological actuality, declares the truth—Harold's need for the loyalty of a woman. This truth is more profound than the one ironically allotted earlier to Sir Edwin. And the narrator's truth is not ironic when he blames Mildred for the catastrophe.

For many years there had been rumors that before World War 1 Forster had started a novel to be called *Arctic Summer*, but had never finished it. In this case, rumor has proved not false. On June 10, 1951, at the Aldeburgh Festival, Forster read a portion of the unfinished novel. In 1963 he permitted the portion to be published, and a note at the end informs us that the fragment was "written in the Spring of 1914." [12]

The fragment is not self-contained and will not pass as a short story, as chapters from works-in-progress sometimes do. Of chief interest is Forster's copious explanation of why he did not finish the novel, an explanation that, as he says, involves us in "fiction-technicalities." [13]

What we are given of the fragment introduces us to four of the major characters, aboard a train in Switzerland. They are Martin Whitby; his wife, Venetia; her mother, Lady Borlase; and a stranger, Lt. C. P. March. The story gets far enough for Lt. March to save Martin from an accident, for some fairly interesting discussion to take place among the family trio, for a conversation to be struck up between Martin and Lt. March, and for Forster to conclude, "Such was the origin of their friendship." [14]

Of particular interest in connection with earlier observations made here concerning Forster as a social thinker is Martin's answer when Lady Borlase asks him whether he expects the "new era" of his generation to be a "dawn." Martin replies, "I should not . . . for the very good reason that my new era is to have no dawn. It is to be a kind of Arctic Summer, in which there will be time to get something really important done. . . . Dawn implies twilight, and we have decided to abolish them both." [15]

The influence of the Bloomsbury group, of its effort to combine an interest in aesthetics with an interest in the social problems of the era, is apparent. "Youth demands colour and blue sky, but Martin, turned thirty, longed for Form. Perhaps it is a cold desire, but it can save many from cynicism; it is a worker's religion, and Italy is one of its shrines." [16] There is more of Ruskin in the bit about Form as the "worker's religion" and "Italy is one of its shrines" than there is of early twentieth-century social realism, but the attempt to make Martin both an aesthete and a democrat is worth noting. The matter is made even more explicit by a passage near the end of the fragment.

> Martin had entered [Italy] often before, but never with such sensations; he saw a quality that he would have despised ten years ago. She, like himself, had abandoned sentiment: she existed apart from associations by the virtues of mass and line: her austere beauty was an image of the millennium towards which all good citizens are cooperating.[17]

These lines, if they are not ironic, read like an attempt to find a common basis for the socialist uprising in Italy in the spring of 1914; the growing coolness of Italy at this crucial historical moment toward her formal ally, Austria; the aesthetic theories of Roger Fry and Clive Bell, and the political-social hopes of the entire Bloomsbury group.[18] Perhaps history, as much as problems in "fiction-technicalities," has something to do with the fact that *Arctic Summer* was never finished. Like certain of the short stories, it seems to have started on an ideational base so broad that the clouds or the skies only, not the earth below, could match it in scope. Although Forster had solved the problem in *A Room with a View* (1908), he had done so by beginning upon a smaller base. It was not until *A Passage to India* that he was able to manage a canvas quite as large and as potentially airy and over diluted as *Arctic Summer* seemed destined to be.

To rediscover him creating fiction out of concrete materials, we are obliged again to go back in time. Four of his completed and published novels appeared between 1905 and 1910. To take up the first in order of publication, *Where Angels Fear to Tread* (1905), after exploring his short stories and *Arctic Summer,* is to emerge from uneven ground, not always solid underfoot, upon a brightly lit landscape, dotted with sharply etched human figures and durable habitations. The movement of the figures weaves an intricate and morally emblazoned fabric—a plot, the form really satisfying to his temperament. For Forster, a plot is not only a structure or shape but a field for the thoughts, feelings, and behavior of "people" and for their relations with each other.

PRAISE OF *Where Angels Fear to Tread*[1] has not been niggardly. Recent critics have agreed for the most part with Lionel Trilling's observation that the novel is "a whole and mature work dominated by a fresh and commanding intelligence."[2] In praising Forster's firm grasp, at the age of twenty-six, of the intellectual possibilities of plot, they have agreed also, "it is a virtue of plot that it keeps the personality of the novelist within bounds," and, "because it is concerned not only with states of being, but with consequences, gives the greatest reality to social forces. It suggests . . . the social connection of individuals."[3] We can add, too, that given Forster's youth when he published *Where Angels Fear to Tread*, we have reason to be perennially astonished by the breadth and intellectual boldness of its themes, the psychological realization of its characters, and the sustained lightness and seriousness of its tone.

Nevertheless, some of the excitement generated by the novel is lost if we do not see an unintended contention between strengths and weaknesses. Its triumph, ultimately only partial, is not only the static sum of the virtues of the novel but also the manner in which it prevails over certain silently wobbling incidents and character traits upon which it often perilously rests its weight.

The story concerns the Herritons of Sawston—Mrs. Herriton, Harriet, and Philip—the first of Forster's middle-class English families whose members finally separate from each other because of the insularity of some and the ability of others to grow. The story has to do also with Lilia, Mrs. Herriton's widowed daughter-in-law; Gino, an Italian she meets and impulsively marries in the little Italian town of Monteriano; and Caroline Abbott, "the first of a series of characters who play a special role throughout Forster's novels. They are his guardians, the medium through which the truth is revealed to those who are capable of understanding it." [4] The pleasure in viewing Forster's five novels together is that one sees how certain characters become reformulated: changing sex, social position, or country; losing or gaining a characteristic; going from flat to round or the reverse.

The plot involves Lilia's marriage to Gino, the birth of her baby boy, her summary death, and what happens when the Herritons, afraid of Caroline Abbott's concern for the baby, decide to get him away from Gino.

Philip and Harriet are dispatched by Mrs. Herriton to negotiate with Gino, who has already been described as avaricious and who did, in fact, marry Lilia partly for her money. But Caroline, who travels independently to save the baby from whatever scheme Mrs. Herriton may have in mind, discovers that Gino's love for his child is authentic and overwhelming. Her discovery is soon shared by Philip. Harriet, however, who is obtuse, insular, and not-to-be-reached, disrupts the new feelings and relationships that have begun to flourish. She kidnaps the baby, who is killed when the escape carriage she has ordered for herself and Philip—the latter ignorant of what she has done—overturns. One of the best scenes in the novel then takes place. Gino, in silent rage, tortures Philip, whose arm was broken in the accident. Caroline appears, and Gino collapses into grief, sobbed out upon her breast.

In the concluding pages, as the train carrying Caroline, Philip, and Harriet approaches the St. Gothard tunnel, into which they will disappear on their retreat from Italy, Philip confesses his love for Caroline, only to learn that she loves the man she will never marry, Gino. She declares that she loves him "crudely," in full, passionate, sexual longing.

Many ideas and themes can be discovered in the intellectual ferment generated by this plot. Two, however, have unusual strength of presence. The first is that characters, engaged with each other in the situations presented in the novel, become engaged also with culture and history. The second is that romance, reserved for a few, easily confused with a "spurious sentiment" superficially resembling it, is, paradoxically in the light of its elitist connotations, essential for all life. A third matter of interest, though not precisely a theme, is the role in the novel of scenes that are, in effect, tableaux.

Part of Forster's talent is an ability to be explicit without being obvious. In this important respect he is like Jane Austen, Dickens, and Thackeray (at his best). Forster's intelligence seems constantly to be winning, without strenuous wrestling, the true perception that lies somewhere between a worn-out idea degenerated into a piety and its too simple refutation or antithesis. His themes are expressed in apposite aphorisms. But instead of remaining static, these aphorisms are points of departure, or promptings along the way, for the energetic drive of the plot toward the full disclosure of what happens when events and ideas impinge upon character.

Lilia, shortly before she gives birth and dies, at first despairs, principally because Gino has been engaging in what are, for him, casual infidelities. Then, gaining for a moment the courage to show her sense of outrage, she confronts him. To Gino, her feelings and behavior are inexplicable. As far as he can see, all that is wrong is that he has been discovered. Confessing, he laughs—admits the joke is upon him—and redoubles his efforts to be kind to Lilia. But she cannot forgive, and pursues her way toward escape—in death. Forster writes, "No one realized that more than personalities were engaged; that the struggle was national; that generations of ancestors, good, bad, or indifferent, forbade the Latin man to be chivalrous to the northern woman, the northern woman to forgive the Latin man." [5]

The statement not only casts both a backward and a final light upon the marriage that has failed but also operates subtly in the action that is to follow. Philip and Caroline will come to Italy. Philip and Gino will discover the possibility of comradeship, despite national and class barriers. Caroline will fall in love with Gino but will be saved by another barrier of nationalism—Gino's inability to comprehend that her love for him is sexual desire. And she will be saved from marriage with Gino, bound to be as disastrous as Lilia's—if for different reasons—by the same essential work of generations in the formation of her character and Gino's.

Another way of approaching the issue is through manners, convention, and morality. Forster knew that in 1905 history and culture encouraged "good manners" to exist between men but set up barriers between women and men of different classes and nationalities. In *Where Angels Fear to Tread*, so strong is the hold of history and culture upon sexual relations that morality must look elsewhere for its relation with manners. The conventional manners of the Sawston Herritons are immoral. They encourage Mrs. Herriton to think she can buy Gino's baby. They lead Harriet into the plainly criminal act of kidnapping the baby. On the other hand, Gino's manners express what is best in him: his capacity for friendship with other men.

More complex are the relations between Caroline's manners and morality, and Philip's. Having already relegated sexual relations to the care of history and culture, Forster can create an identity between Caroline's manners and morality, in the latter part of the novel, without running risks he wishes to avoid. After Caroline has seen Gino with his baby, her developing vision of truth is expressed in her manners. The phenomenon makes her wise, beautiful, and desirable; and both Gino and Philip worship her as a goddess.

In Gino's case, the adoration is the result of culture and history. His customary view of women, and his structured behavior toward them, will not do in the case of this heroine; therefore Forster encourages Gino's Mediterranean imagination to put her beyond reach. But what of

Philip? When he has reached full development, his manners express cognizance of moral truth. Why, then, cannot
Caroline accept him as a husband in the place of the
unacceptable Gino?

There are many possible answers, and among them is to
be found the weaknesses of the novel. But one positive
answer is that the fully awakened Caroline at the end of
the novel has learned that actions matter, that they do
have consequences. In the action of the final episode
Philip, although morally awake too, has played too feminine and passive a role. He has "seen" all that Caroline
has seen; but he has seen no more. He has not seen what
would have been beyond her ken: how, concretely, to deal
with Harriet in a masculine manner before the tragedy
occurs. With foreboding, Caroline had urged Philip to get
Harriet out of Monteriano, shortly before the kidnapping.
Had Philip done so, and on his own initiative, the "mystery" surrounding Caroline would have been transferred to
him—in Caroline's eyes. Referring to the earlier part of
the novel, to the marriage of Lilia and Gino, Lionel
Trilling has noted that the situation is reminiscent of D.
H. Lawrence's *The Lost Girl*, but that Lawrence "was to
evoke a complex and triumphant sexuality," whereas "Forster's Lilia is not sexual . . . ." [6] In Lawrence's sense, Philip lacks sexuality, too, despite his moral courage in facing
Gino after the tragedy of the baby's death and despite his
ability to declare his love, at the end of the novel. For
Caroline, he continues to the end of the novel to lack
"mystery," male mystery.

"Mystery" suggests, too, the second theme of the novel,
romance. The latter replaces the myth and fantasy of the
short stories, and Forster gives it breadth and scope. A
variety of human experiences are associated with romance,
an energizing theme in the creation of character and plot.

Recognition of the true meaning of romance, of its
relationship to the fully lived life, is given to the ultimately defeated Philip. At the beginning of the novel,
when Lilia is about to set out for Italy, Philip tells "her of
the supreme moments of her coming journey—the Cam-

panile of Airolo, which would burst on her when she emerged from the St. Gothard tunnel, presaging the future" (*p. 8*). Not only is this romantic rendering of the moment of passage into Italy to be taken seriously — Forster was prepared in the unfinished *Arctic Summer* to make the same tunnel bear much serious meaning — but Philip's words to Lilia bring us directly to the structure of the plot. At the very end of the novel, when Caroline says that "all the wonderful things are over," the "train was crawling up the last ascent towards the Campanile of Airolo and the entrance of the tunnel" (*p. 199*).

Again, at the beginning of the novel, Phillip thinks of Lilia setting out for Italy. "He found the situation full of whimsical romance: there was something half-attractive, half-repellent in the thought of this vulgar woman journeying to places he loved and revered. Why should she not be transfigured? The same had happened to the Goths" (*p. 12*). Once again a reference to romance by Philip will work itself out in characterization and plot, though ironically. It is he, not Lilia, who will become transfigured in Italy.

His reaction to the news he receives from Caroline, that Lilia is to marry Gino, the son of a provincial Italian dentist, is pertinent. "False teeth and laughing gas . . . at a place which knew the Etruscan League, and the Pax Romana, and Alaric himself, . . . and the Middle Ages, all fighting and holiness, and the Renaissance, all fighting and beauty! . . . He was anxious for himself: he feared that Romance might die" (*p. 32*). Forster continues: "Romance only dies with life. . . . But there is a spurious sentiment which cannot resist the unexpected and the incongruous and the grotesque. A touch will loosen it, and the sooner it goes . . . the better. It was going from Philip now, and therefore he gave the cry of pain" (*pp. 32–33*).

Forster should not have suggested that the "spurious sentiment" departs completely from Philip. When Philip later turns Caroline into a "goddess," the consequences suggest that Caroline, at least, associates Philip's lack of masculinity and male mystery with the presence in him of feelings akin to the "spurious sentiment." Contradictions, whoever's hobgoblins they may be, ought not to suggest a lapse in characterization, or a momentary casualness, in the process, that has no purpose.

But as spokesman for romance, even if he remains a dubious actor in its behalf, Philip continues to enlarge, up to a point, its definition. In England, before the second descent upon Monteriano, he tells Caroline, "Society *is* invincible—to a certain degree. But your real life is your own, and nothing can touch it. There is no power on earth that can prevent your criticizing and despising mediocrity —nothing that can stop you retreating into splendour and beauty—into the thoughts and beliefs that make the real life—the real you" (*p.* 89).

There are complex plot associations in this speech. For the true romantic, "retreat" should be only a prelude to action. Philip learns this too late to win the love of Caroline. Caroline, on the other hand, benefits from the partial truth available to Philip. By convincing her that her life is her own, he liberates her to go beyond himself. She sees that "retreat" is not the fulfilment of her identity or his.

When Philip realizes that Mrs. Herriton is scheming to get Lilia's baby away from Gino, he has another moment of insight. "And though [Mrs. Herriton] was frightening him, she did not inspire him with reverence. Her life, he saw, was without meaning. To what purpose was her diplomacy, her insincerity, her continued repression of vigour? Did they make anyone better or happier? Did they even bring happiness to herself? Harriet with her gloomy peevish creed, Lilia with her clutches after pleasure, were after all more divine than this well-ordered, active, useless machine" (*p.* 98).

Insight without action. The paralysis, only occasionally painful, characterizes Philip when Forster is associating him with romance. Forster eventually seems to become aware of the problem, and he attempts to establish a consistent role for Philip. But he does so at the expense of Philip's masculinity and in seemingly approving language, at odds with Caroline's insight into Philip. Nevertheless, there would have been nothing wrong with Forster's resolution of character if the authorial voice had not intruded. Unconsciously, Forster sets himself, not Philip, in opposition to Caroline. Even though he does so only intermittently, Forster's unwitting conflict with her over the proper view of Philip becomes another instance of a casualness having no proper place in characterization.

Forster establishes Philip's role and permits himself to judge—unfortunately—while describing Philip's second arrival in Monteriano. During his first visit, Philip had been rudely pushed by Gino. Ordered by Mrs. Herriton to buy Lilia's baby, eighteen months later, Philip, reaching Monteriano, is greeted by Caroline. Shocked and angered at first by her interference, he succumbs with remarkable ease when she tells him something of no obviously large importance: that Gino is sorry for his past rudeness to him. "Philip smiled . . . . This admirable change in Philip . . . may . . . provoke the gibes of the cynical. But angels and other practical people will . . . write it down as good" (p. 125).

In the context, Forster's allusion to the novel's title is more suggestive than we have any warrant to suppose was his deliberate intention. Caroline will tread where Philip fears to go. The patron saint of Monteriano, Santa Deodata, refused on earth to partake in action, for she believed that "retreat" was her pious calling. After her death, however, remembrance of her inspired the townspeople to heroic deeds. So, too, Caroline, awakened by Philip, will act. She will not, however, approve of Philip's inability to anticipate her, and since she is the most liberated of the characters, Forster's calling upon angels and other practical folk to testify in behalf of Philip comes near to creating a double viewpoint in the novel. In assigning to Philip the role of unmoved mover, Forster would have done better to mute and make more tacit his approbation of Philip's essentially feminine function. He would have done even better had he refrained, in the process of assigning Philip his destiny, from all authorial judgment. Not the least gained would have been a clearer sense of

Philip's authentic contribution to the elaboration, within the novel, of romance as a theme and idea.

Caroline's vision is an expanded view of romance's ethical meaning. Other amplifications of romance are Forster's treatment of the beautiful—in Italy at the turn of the century—and of Gino's paternal pride.

One of the novel's finest scenes includes a description of Monteriano's opera house. Through Forster's tone, viewpoint, and instinct for detail, beauty becomes a fresh concept, newly vital and alluring. And in this concept, moreover, humor—the extravagant and grotesque—contend with romance. The latter wins.

Years earlier, prior to the events encompassed by the novel, Philip had visited the opera house. In the interval, the theater "had been thoroughly done up, in the tints of the beetroot and the tomato . . . . Some of the boxes had terra-cotta draperies . . . . There was also a drop-scene, representing a pink and purple landscape, wherein sported many a lady lightly clad, and two more ladies lay along the top of the proscenium to steady a large and pallid clock. . . . There is something majestic in the bad taste of Italy. . . . It observes beauty, and chooses to pass it by. But it attains to beauty's confidence" (*p.* 131).

For Forster, nothing is closer to the heart of true romance than "beauty's confidence," and the phrase is striking. "Confidence" leads to action and moral consequences. Forster has not only used humor to revitalize the idea of beauty but has, with startling and only seeming casualness, opened a window on a whole field of speculation about the link between aesthetics and morality.

To suggest a path in that field, he has Gino, who, with a group of friends, is present at a performance attended by Philip, Harriet, and Caroline, comically but warmly express brotherliness for Philip, when the Englishman is discovered in the audience. The recognition, accompanied by affectionate antics, interleaves with other aspects of the relationship between Gino and Philip and establishes the ground for the important episodes between them yet to occur.

Gino enlarges the compass of romance when Lilia, pregnant with his son, begins the decline that will end in her death in childbirth. She takes to her bed, months before the baby is due. Gino is distracted. "His one desire was to become the father of a man like himself, and it held him with a grip he only partially understood, for it was the first great desire, the first great passion of his life. Falling in love was a mere physical triviality . . . beside this divine hope of immortality: 'I continue' " (*pp.* 76–77). This is romance. Forster might have assigned Gino's desire for fatherhood, like his manners and morality toward women, to history and culture. But associating Gino's dream of fatherhood with romance is accurate, within the thematic context of the novel. To be a fully realized and "realistic" concept, romance must include the instinctual life. Only Gino, among the major characters, lives this life consistently and with natural depth. Gino and his dream-ambition add another dimension to romance, rooting it in the blood and the earth.

Gino's relation to his son continues to be an aspect of romance. Caroline visits Gino and realizes for the first time that he loves his child: "She was silent. . . . The horrible truth, that wicked people are capable of love, stood naked before her . . . . It was her duty to rescue the baby . . . and she . . . meant to do [it]. But the comfortable sense of virtue left her. She was in the presence of something greater than right or wrong" (*p.* 152).

Her recognition that the wicked can love recalls "The Story of the Siren." Caroline's sense that Gino's love for his child is beyond right and wrong gives the love a dimension and aura beyond history and social fact. And a moment later, watching Gino holding the baby, Caroline invests the scene with definitive meaning. "The man was majestic; he was a part of Nature; in no ordinary love scene could he ever be so great" (*p.* 155). Although only an onlooker, she advances from what she has already learned from Philip's truth and lecturing. She becomes a priestess of the something beyond right and wrong.

In her new awareness, she becomes intent upon weaving the plot. It is now that she urges Philip to take Harriet away before something terrible happens. She speaks of the large consequences of small actions and inactions. Her attempt to direct the plot, however, is unsuccessful, a fact that is further testimony to Forster's skill. Because Caroline is a woman in a land and at a time when history prevents women from acting, she fails to avert the tragedy—the baby's death when Harriet kidnaps the child and the escape carriage overturns.

Caroline's defeat by history, by the fact that she is only a woman, is the first of Forster's successful and subtle transformations, in his novels, that take place as a means of relating character, plot, and theme. Forster's technique is akin to varying the key in music. To create a new morality in Caroline, Forster removes her from history and exposes her to the truth of romance. However, once she has, as a consequence, acquired vision and the consequent desire to act, he reintroduces history and puts it in contention with her new morality. The second is bound to lose. Historic realism, retaining its more effective control of plot, requires that the encounter end in the defeat and surrender of her upstart morality.

Romance, nevertheless, endures as a theme despite the degree of direction over plot exercised by history. Except in Caroline's case, which, in this connection must be viewed in its entirety and in retrospect, the truth of romance, meant by Forster to be a force in the novel, in no other respect meets the force of history in a head-on challenge. Romance works its will in the gaps and declivities untouched by the cumbrous activity of history. Yet such is the nature of romance that it can enrich itself on the stuff of history, even as it avoids the problems of realism and plot that a challenge for supremacy of truth would precipitate.

In the last tableau of the novel, Caroline, returned to romance and permitted to act, combines, with it, the "something" beyond, although she has not prevented the tragedy. The baby is dead. Philip, who had been duped by Harriet and had been in the carriage when it overturned, who had thought that Gino had willingly relinquished his child, has bravely returned to tell Gino what has happened. Philip is unmindful of his arm, broken in the accident. Gino, still in shock, turns on Philip. Concentrating on the broken arm, the Italian is in the process of torturing the Englishman to death. Caroline arrives and breaks the spell of silent murder. Clasping her, Gino at last begins to sob out his grief.

> All through the day Miss Abbott had seemed to Philip like a goddess, and more than ever did she seem so now. . . . Her eyes were . . . full of infinite pity and . . . majesty, as if they discerned the boundaries of sorrow, and saw unimaginable tracts beyond. Such eyes he had seen in great pictures but never in a mortal. . . . It seemed fitting, too, that she should bend her head and touch [Gino's] forehead with her lips.
>
> Philip looked away, as he sometimes [did] from the great pictures where visible forms suddenly became inadequate for the things they have shown to us. . . . There came to him an earnest desire to be good through the example of this good woman. . . . Quietly, . . . he underwent conversion. He was saved (*p. 192*).

Romance has here embraced allegory. Caroline is the Madonna, not only for Philip but for Gino, although the Italian's response suggests his unintellectualized faith while Philip's vision implies a cultured imagination touched by mystical but secularly rooted sympathies.

In writing of this scene, John Beer not only crosses the boundary between history and romance but alludes to Forster's humanistic creed, "Forster is using two of his favourite visionary modes—Italian renaissance painting and Greek mythology—to express his own form of humanism. . . . [that] includes the realism which works . . . against social abuses but regards this as unfulfilled unless it . . . can see humanity as touched with glory." [7]

Forster's humanism has not figured in the present analysis of the novel, and for a particular reason. Humanism can, of course, be seen in the good will that develops in Philip and Caroline, as well as in the portrait of Gino. But it was not until Forster had finished *A Room*

with a View, published in 1908 but actually begun in
1903, that he resolved a humanistic problem touched on
in *Where Angels Fear to Tread* and implicit in the tableau seen through Philip's eyes. At least part of the
realism in the scene is sexuality, although we do not learn
the fact until the last chapter. Although Philip, both for
reasons pertaining to Forster's characterization of him and
Forster's own inability, in this novel, to reconcile sex and
humanism, does not see it, when Caroline later confesses
that she loves Gino "crudely" (*p. 201*), she casts a
retrospective meaning upon the tableau. Sorrow dominated, but her kiss expressed sexual desire.

However blind to the fact Philip may be, her desire
raises two questions. Why did Forster, instead of permitting humanism to include fulfilled sexuality, choose a
novelistically simpler solution—Caroline's return to Sawston and an implication that she will lead a sexless life?
And what, as a related matter, happens to romance as a
theme when it is revealed as based, in some manifestations, on repressed or diverted sexuality? They are
questions which would not have been necessary had Forster kept in focus his initial, wise decision to relegate
sexuality to history.

Part of the answer is that romance *has* at least formed
Caroline's morality and awakened her sexuality. Romance
was never meant to provide her with a husband—only
history could do that. Moreover, when, in the last chapter,
she declares to Philip her love for Gino, she adds, " 'If I
saw him often . . . I might remember what he is like. Or
he might grow old. But I dare not risk it, so nothing can
alter me now' " (*p. 202*). She has expressed a realistic fear
of history, which had made Gino the kind of husband to
Lilia that Caroline will sensibly avoid. Nevertheless, her
words also indicate that she regards her love for Gino as
an "eternal moment," a less satisfactory concept here than
in the story of Miss Raby or in Forster's next novel, *The
Longest Journey* (1907), where it is expertly introduced
and explored. Because Caroline's resignation and return to
Sawston follow her "eternal moment," Forster is no longer

attempting to liberate "the undeveloped heart," [8] to add to romance the vitality of sex.

The same process is evident in the ultimate characterization of Philip, but by a curious luck of circumstance, inherent in the creative act, Forster's imperiling the theme of romance by failing to reconcile or align it with sexuality results in the resolution, in the last moments of the novel, of Philip's role. Philip has been "saved" by a woman who cannot save herself. When, at the conclusion, he proposes to Caroline and she summarily rejects him, speaking of her love for Gino, the canvas is cleared for the mark and emphasis that are finally to stabilize Philip.

He acquires the goddess virtue of enlarged vision. He sees not only "the boundaries of sorrow, and [the] unimaginable tracts beyond"; he sees the plot of *Where Angels Fear to Tread*. " 'But through my fault,' " he tells Caroline, Gino " 'is parted from the child he loves. And because my life was in danger you came . . . to him again.' For the thing was even greater than she imagined. Nobody but himself would ever see round it now. And to see round it he was standing at an immense distance. He could even be glad that she had once held the beloved in her arms" (*pp. 203–4*).

Nevertheless, this concluding clarification of Philip, by depriving him of all masculinity (realistically, his "vision" is a startling response to his rejection when he proposes marriage to a woman), discloses a new peril to the theme that romance is a form of truth. Romance is effectively challenged in the novel by history and imperiled by its unresolved relation to sexuality. As a further consequence of the latter, unintended fact, romance is endangered by the inevitable suggestion that it has been fed by the imagination produced by repression—in Caroline's case, as well as in Philip's. Both characters, we realize, have been able to give but not to receive. As a result, an undesirable shadow becomes noticeable even in the authentic new morality and activism with which romance has endowed Caroline.

To an extent, Gino's contribution to the theme of romance compensates for the weaknesses, unresolved problems, and unintended implications in the characterizations of Caroline and Philip. But the vividness of his compensatory presence also poses a new problem—the unequal balance, in the novel, between Italy and England.

Gino is able both to give and to receive. His love of his son is an authentic element in the composite truth of romance. Had his "male mystery" been evident to a less contradictory and complicated woman than Caroline, he would have been a Lawrentian figure and would have greatly enriched the theme of romance. Nevertheless, from the authorial viewpoint, his sexuality, though casual and unimportant to Gino himself, influences the development of the English so strongly as to claim to be a minor enlargement of romance.

However, Forster's emphatic and consistent characterization of Gino gives Italy, through association, weight and importance, leaving England, in comparison, far behind. Even without Gino's presence, Italy, in the novel, is the land of romance. Including him also means a constant awareness of the distinction between Gino and the English and of the unfavorable and thin treatment of England.

It may be true that "Forster is not taken in by his Gino . . . and if he defends Mediterranean instinct against British cant or phlegm, he knows the limits of its value." [9] It may also be correct, in regarding the novel as one about "a conflict between two worlds, as represented by . . . Sawston . . . and . . . Monteriano . . . . Forster . . . avoided oversimplification in his opposition of these two places, these two ways of life: he turned the full dry light of social comedy on Monteriano as well as on Sawston." [10] But Gino's capacity for cruelty, his almost mystical love for his baby, his ability to inspire love in Caroline have a power matched by Philip and Caroline in only one scene: Gino's attempt to kill a temporarily brave Philip and the consequent deification of a compassionate Caroline by both men. And the more prosaic fact that most of the scenes take place in Monteriano gives the weight to Italy, the Middle Ages, and the Renaissance.

We are too acutely reminded that Sawston society has only a few generations of tradition behind it, and we are not sufficiently made aware that this unattractive tradition has a certain strength lent by even a relatively brief historical heritage or by Sawston's participation in the longer and larger tradition of all Britain.

The inequality further adulterates the theme of romance. "Since the Renaissance . . . it had been a device of moralists to confront their own culture with the superior habits of foreign lands. And in the 19th century . . . it became possible to see for oneself whether they really did order these things better in France—or in Italy. . . . The charm . . . found was no doubt sentimental, but it was also moral. An unknown people is not only quaint but also good." [11] When this observation is applied to *Where Angels Fear to Tread*, however, "quaint" becomes a newly vitiating point of view upon romance, surely unintended by Forster.

Furthermore, there is another tradition—established by the English Romantic poets, who traveled equally on the Continent and in the country of the mind's imagination, even, in the latter, back to the Middle Ages and the Renaissance. But Forster does not permit them to create a background in depth for Caroline and Philip and therefore, by extension, for England.

It is, of course, Forster's privilege to have made the contest between Italy and England unequal. And some of his conscious purposes require him to do so. Nevertheless, part of the inequality is associated with the unresolved consequences of Caroline's transfiguration by romance, and it is just possible that had Forster given England more substance, even at the cost of sacrificing part of the intentional primacy of Italy, he would have seen a way to resolve the problems inherent in the characterization of Caroline. He had, after all, wisely at first relegated sex to history, not romance.

Since he did not retain the separation, or successfully meet the new challenges once sex had been tested in the realm of romance, he obliges us to step outside the novel and see that history and culture have actually made the north and south of Europe equal contestants, even, perhaps, in romance. And what is relevant is that he obliges us to disregard what we see when we take the step outside the novel. Only by ignoring our independently arrived at view of Europe's history can we see that the haplessness of Philip and Caroline, and the peevishness of Harriet, are inevitable, at the novel's conclusion, as the train carrying the English disappears into the San Gotthard tunnel, on its way north and west.

"THE LONGEST JOURNEY is the least popular of my five novels but the one I am most glad to have written," Forster wrote in 1960.[1] In recent years, he has been so obligingly explicit about the meaning of *The Longest Journey* that the critic who admires it has been in an odd position: he has been required to reconcile his own reading of the novel with the explanatory statements Forster has supplied. But though presenting difficulties, the position is neither false nor valueless. The dialectic at the heart of any critical enterprise—the dialogue between the text and the reader's response to it—has merely been enriched by the introduction of a third element: Forster's glosses upon his own work.

Forster has published some of his preliminary notes for *The Longest Journey*. He speaks of a diary entry for July 18, 1904: "An idea for another novel—that of a man who discovers that he has an illegitimate brother." However, during the interval between 1904 and 1907 "several other ideas intervened to confuse or enrich the original theme. There was the metaphysical idea of Reality ('the cow is there'): . . . the ethical idea that reality must be faced (Rickie won't face Stephen); . . . the idea, or ideal, of the British Public School; . . . the title, exhorting us in the words of Shelley not to love one person only; there was Cambridge, there was Wiltshire." [2]

The Longest Journey concerns Rickie Elliot, an imaginative youth who, in the course of the story, moves from his last three years as a Cambridge undergraduate; through a disastrous marriage to Agnes Pembroke, including a miserable life as a teacher in Sawston School; where her brother, an influential master, has obtained a position for him; to Rickie's death in Wiltshire, which occurs because he saves the life of his half brother, Stephen Wonham, but is too weary to save himself. Stephen is an important figure. In his character and actions are caught up much of what Forster wants to say about England's past—both historical and mysterious—about Nature, and about truthfulness. Moreover, in his relation to England's past, Stephen is an unintentional resolution of some of the unintended problems in *Where Angels Fear to Tread.*

Truthfulness characterizes another central figure, Stewart Ansell. He is Rickie's friend in Cambridge. Approaching truth through the metaphysical problem of Reality, he puts himself in touch with the moral and concrete actualities of life: friendship, ethical conduct, and the problem of individual identity. When Rickie has gone morally bankrupt—has become a catspaw of Agnes and her brother Herbert and has passively joined them in denying and concealing the fact that Rickie and Stephen are half brothers—Ansell rescues Rickie from a tangle of lost identity and immorality and makes possible the relationship between Rickie and Stephen that dominates the third section of the novel. And we learn that after Rickie's death Stephen and Ansell have become fast friends.

Certain characters who have died before the novel begins influence the living: Mrs. Elliot (Rickie's and Stephen's mother); Mr. Elliot, Rickie's hated father, who has passed on to Rickie an hereditary deformed foot and who abuses and almost kills Mrs. Elliot's capacity for love; Mr. Failing, an intellectual Wiltshire squire who combines knowledge of nature with a concern for personal relations; and Robert, a Wiltshire farmer who rescues Mrs. Elliot from her loveless life and who fathers Stephen.

Without a last name, like the Saxons of old, Robert is the logical father of his son. His intuitive knowledge of the earth anticipates Stephen's. But he is articulate about his nature experience, while Stephen is not.

The reason for this difference between the two is the logic of plot. Robert is self-sufficient. Like an eternal moment, he is a complete man, brought briefly into the story to fulfill his important mission. Stephen is incomplete. More central in the story, he must raise questions about personal relations. And through these he ultimately gains a degree of Robert's verbal ease (actually through Ansell's teaching and Rickie's spiritual and material legacy).

The themes of the novel arise out of Rickie's poetic imagination; Ansell's intellectual search for truth and his moral action; and Stephen's relation to the earth, the past, and living people. The themes arise also out of the negation and denial of truth and goodness on the part of Herbert, Agnes, and Mrs. Failing (Rickie's aunt). On a broader scale, these themes are conventional society in early twentieth-century England, the meaning and value of England's history and tradition, and the connotations of the question, what is Reality?

When the novel opens a group of Cambridge undergraduates are discussing an old metaphysical problem: is a cow "real"—does it exist—if no one is there to see it? Ansell, usually at home with abstract and abstruse problems, oddly casts aside logic and the necessity for proof. He says that the cow *is* there, and when challenged for evidence, answers solipsistically, "She's there for me. . . . Whether I'm in Cambridge or Iceland or dead, the cow will be there." [3] Ansell has spurned his own ability to engage in mental gymnastics, to play, in compliance with the rules, the game of logic. This is precisely Forster's moral point and method for establishing Ansell and his role in the novel.

Ansell will, as the novel develops, declare that truthfulness in human relations is possible, as is action in its behalf. But for truth to be possible and actual, people must be real. Fully conscious of what he is doing, Ansell has abandoned method and logic in order to assert the reality of his own identity—an identity without which perception of the truth or falsehood in human relations, as well as the ability to act morally, would be impossible. If the cow is real, whether anyone sees her or not, so, too, is Ansell. His nonlogical faith in the cow's existence is an analogue for his nonlogical belief in himself and his values.

Rickie's response to the problem of the cow—the problem of reality—is different.

> Was she there or not? . . . If she was there, other cows were there too. . . . Yet . . . suppose the cow not to be there unless oneself was there to see her. A cowless world, then, stretched round him. . . . Yet he had only to peep into a field, and, click! it would at once become radiant with bovine life. . . .
>
> As usual, he . . . was overlaying philosophy with gross and senseless details (*pp.* 8–9).

Lionel Trilling points to the relevance, in the larger world, of Rickie's imagination, "reality is a more exact concept than truth and simple people are more interested in it than in truth; reality . . . is what is thick, and lasts." [4] In *The Longest Journey*, however, the truth is elusive and difficult to explore through critical methods. It can be done, but by narrowing, even at times eliminating, Trilling's distinction between "reality" and "truth."

At Cambridge Rickie reads classics and receives a "creditable second." Ansell reads Moral Science and receives a first. Rickie's classicism seems inferior to Ansell's Moral Science, but Forster creates a deliberate ambivalence. Rickie's classicism is the poetic and romantic aspect of reality. Its deference to Moral Science is both necessary and ironic. It is necessary because poetic imagination and romanticism not only will fail to solve problems that Ansell's personalized "moral science" can, but will make Rickie the victim of what Ansell calls "diseased imagination" (*p.* 24). It is ironic because it will disclose aspects of the truth unknown to any other kind of imagination.

This is not to say that the life of the poetic imagination

does not have its perils. The novel is quite explicit about what these are. But every life in *The Longest Journey* is beset by perils, and if Rickie at fateful times is weaker or more in error than the other "good" characters, his true perceptions are never cancelled; his weakness and errors do not follow deterministically from the fact that his sensibility is poetic and romantic.

The romantic, the poetically imaginative, is not only a theme in the novel, it is part of Forster's technique. In Rickie's room at Cambridge hang a number of pictures. Among them are a view of Stockholm and a portrait of Rickie's mother. As the novel progresses, the picture of Stockholm becomes a symbol—a "thing" made poetic. Stockholm is the city where Stephen was conceived. The picture reappears in Dunwood House at Sawston School, during the worst period in Rickie's life. In the third section of the novel, Stephen Wonham, after Rickie's death, transfers the picture to his own house in Wiltshire. The other picture, of Rickie's mother, also travels from Cambridge to Dunwood House, but there it is torn to pieces by Stephen.

The introduction of these two photographs, for poetic reasons, suggests the true deficiency in Rickie. His romantic imagination, as such, does not cause tragedy; his fatal propensity to turn people into symbols does. The romantic imagination is correct in perceiving symbolism in things, i.e., the picture of Stockholm, but not in people, living or dead. Rickie's weakness is an inability to see when poetry does not apply to personal relations.

In some ways he is the reverse of Caroline Abbott, who, despite her deficiencies, sees the romantic imagination's limits after one experience. Rickie never learns. Yet curiously, both suffer the same consequence: loss of hope. Neither novel makes clear whether Forster, who believes in the humane uses of reason, also believes that a poetic imagination gone wrong is amenable to reason. Whether pessimism, conception of plot, or some unexpressed understanding of the irrational guides his hand, the romantic imagination, in his first two published novels, defeats itself. *The Longest Journey*, however, takes up this sad fact where the earlier novel drops it. And the fact becomes transformed into a theme, fully explored.

Early in the novel, Rickie sees the unimaginative couple—Agnes Pembroke and Gerald—kiss. He realizes that morally unattractive people are capable of love. But Rickie disengages his perception from the actors who make it possible. The observed kiss becomes, for him, a "symbolic moment," proof against consequences, associated with infinite time rather than with daily life.

The Longest Journey is filled with symbolic moments, as well as symbolic things. The former are invariably good, which means to Forster that they can hold their own among alien truths and even have the power to correct unmitigated lies. For example, Gerald suddenly and unexpectedly dies. Agnes is in a perilous state. She has never learnt to grieve, and the people surrounding her offer assurances that Gerald is in the Christian heaven. But Rickie forces her to see that her engagement is over, transformed into an eternal moment: complete but unable to console. She breaks down and sobs out her authentic grief. Rickie's poetic truth has saved her from the threatening unreality of those who insist that Gerald is not "really" gone.

But Rickie loses his clear vision of his own kind of truth. He falls in love with Agnes. He forgets that he has been entranced by the kiss Agnes and Gerald exchanged, and not by either person. Moreover, he had already made one serious error. He had transformed his dead mother into a symbol. He makes a second mistake, transforming the living Agnes into an equally dangerous symbol. The damage completed, he marries her—marries a girl not only of his own creation but one whom his true poetic power had previously assessed correctly.

These facts anticipate some of the novel's events, although *The Longest Journey*, ostensibly adhering to the three-part division often favored by Forster, weaves the most sinuous and impressionistically constructed of his plots. The novel is divided into "Cambridge," "Sawston," and "Wiltshire," but characters and events important to these places appear constantly throughout, and without regard for the formal divisions. Yet *The Longest Journey* is controlled by a structure paradoxically both rough and intimately suggestive. Important Cambridge scenes do occur in Part I. Somewhere in the midst of "Sawston" Rickie marries Agnes. And Wiltshire events do predominate in Part III, though similar and anticipatory episodes occur frequently before the final section.

Much has been written about the Cambridge scenes, which at least accent Part I. Forster is not as detailed as his commentators, but his 1960 reminiscences provide a succinct summary. And in a discussion of his novels, no opportunity to hear his tone or be reminded of his style and personality should be neglected. "Cambridge is the home of Rickie, the elder brother, the legitimate, his only true home: the Cambridge of G. E. Moore which I knew at the beginning of the century: [5] the fearless uninfluential Cambridge that sought for reality and cared for truth. Ansell is the undergraduate high-priest of that local shrine. . . . The Cambridge chapters are still romantic . . . and I still endorse Ansell's denunciation of the Great World." [6] Forster, in his remark about Ansell, is referring to the latter's reproof of Rickie, when he is leaving Cambridge for Agnes and Sawston School.

> There is no great world . . . the . . . earth is full of tiny societies, and Cambridge is one of them. . . . The good [ones] say, 'I tell you to do this because I am Cambridge.' The bad ones say, 'I tell you to do that because I am the great world, . . .' And fools like you . . . confuse 'great,' which has no meaning . . . with 'good,' which means salvation (*p.* 74).

In *Where Angels Fear to Tread*, Caroline was "good," Philip was "saved." Neither, however, could fully and effectively act. Ansell, however, who doesn't bother to apply these words to himself—he uses them only to describe society—not only will demonstrate that he is both "good" and "saved." He will act, bringing moral conviction and intelligence to bear upon an important plot juncture. He is reminiscent of Meredith's holy triad—blood, brain, and spirit. In Forster's writing, he is an attempted advance beyond Philip Herriton. Ansell, who has already used solipsism for a moral purpose, is out to prove the absence of conflict between the truly trained, flexible intellect and the heart and the will. Like all Forster's characters, he is a tentative position in a search for the possible virtues and achievements of humanism. However, as a figure within the particular novel, *The Longest Journey*, he achieves permanency, whatever its merits. He is the voice of one of the novel's various kinds of truth, he is a plot mover, and he is even capable of further development through personal relations.

His speech to Rickie about society is characteristic of his kind of truth. Another kind is Forster's own. When Rickie, deaf to Ansell, has become fully entangled with Agnes, Herbert, and Sawston School, Forster makes an ambitious effort to confront Ansell's insight with another. The "primal curse," he says, is not knowledge of good and evil but of good-and-evil (*p. 194*).

Sawston School and Herbert are initially portrayed through the moral ambivalence of the "curse." Forster's long description of the school's history and tradition is not entirely unsympathetic, and bringing his assessment to the present, Forster writes, "Where traditions served [the School] clung to them. Where new departures seemed desirable, they were made. It aimed at producing the average Englishman, and, to a very great extent, it succeeded" (*p. 52*).[7]

The literal meaning, as well as the tone of these words, surely suggests good-and-evil rather than any other moral concept. Herbert also is initially characterized by the "primal curse"—in other words, in a way that discourages moral judgment. He "has the will to be good but the undeveloped heart prevents him." [8] The worst that can be said of him is Rickie's unspoken thought: he is stupid. In a man who has power over young lives, stupidity is evil, yet Forster's early view of Herbert continues to be detached and morally evasive, "It is not clear whether his head diminishes his heart or his heart his head." [9] Herbert is both victimizer and victim, potentially a complex figure who might have been consistently characterized by good-and-evil.

Unfortunately, plot requirements apparently obliged Forster, as the novel progressed, to simplify not only Herbert, but Sawston School as well, into unqualified evil. Had the initial characterizations been maintained, Forster would have had to cope with more problems, but he might have achieved new insights into the psychology and morality of his cherished theme, personal relations. He might have submitted them to the operation of good-and-evil on a scale large enough to include all the characters in the novel.

But this is speculation. The fact is that Herbert becomes a direct confirmation of the evil seen by Ansell. Herbert pompously declares, "School . . . is the world in miniature" (*p. 178*). He distorts reality. He tells lies about it. Confident that his morality not only governs the "great world" but does so righteously, he rules his part of Sawston School through snobbery, deceit, and mean politics. He offends against the truthfulness and respect that ought to govern personal relations. Finally, he exploits Rickie's confusion and weakness, changing Rickie, the poetic visionary, into a will-less running dog, who cannot resist doing Herbert's dirtiest political work.

To see Agnes properly, we must return to the beginning of the novel. Her evil, unlike her brother's, is never even tentatively qualified, except through her genuine love for Gerald. Visiting Rickie in his college rooms [in "Cambridge," Part I], she immediately introduces into the novel the popularized, brutal social-Darwinism of the late nineteenth and early twentieth centuries. In doing so, she characterizes herself.

Rickie has a deformed foot, inherited from his father. In literature, he compares with Philip Cary, of Maugham's *Of Human Bondage*. In both literature and psychology, he can be associated with Oedipus. The literal Greek meaning of *oedipus* is "swollen foot." [10] Besides his deformed foot, Rickie has an attachment to his mother that eventually destroys him. Finally, Rickie's foot is a test of character for Agnes. She fails it, just as a large part of middle-class England, at the time, would have.

Agnes is repelled by the hereditary deformation that Rickie bears, and she wonders why he isn't like other people. She is afraid of the different and, by logical extension, of any manifestation of individual identity that threatens her life-denying addiction to mythic stereotypes.

Out of the Wordsworthian creed that nature is good, Agnes and her kind have constructed a distorted and socially repressive morality. Ignorant of what the "natural" is, they denounce any deviation from their superficial concept of it.

Thus Rickie is not simply different; he is, to Agnes, abnormal: "She had known Rickie for many years, but it seemed so dreadful and so different now that he was a man. It was her first great contact with the abnormal, and unknown fibers of her being rose in revolt against it" (*pp.* 17–18).

What also revolts is her conditioned sexuality, a singular attribute of her social Darwinism. Forster condemns and punishes her for this trait and in the process exploits it fully, relating it to other defects in her character and making her pay for their consequences. Her defects are deformations of character that make her more unnatural than Rickie's deformed foot ever causes him to appear or act. Moreover, her social Darwinism is, for Forster, a manifestation also of impoverished imagination. And since her conditioned sexuality is the result of this creed, however oblivious she is to its historical actuality, she is also sexually unimaginative. As a result, after her early revulsion, she marries Rickie, a man she does not love but one who will presumably submit to all expressions of her deformed character. Whether she has any real inkling of why she marries him, her apparent reasons are practical and nothing more. And because of all the associated traits and motives that enable her to marry for these reasons—marry a man she does not love—Forster will punish her.

Before he does however—before she marries Rickie—

Forster further accentuates the cruelty of her social Darwinism. He does so while Gerald is still alive. Gerald had been a schoolmate of Rickie's. When, reminiscing, he laughingly confesses to Agnes that he had bullied Rickie, she "had a thrill of joy when she thought of the weak boy in the clutches of the strong one" (*pp.* 60–61).

In addition, before Agnes is thwarted, Rickie suffers for having married her. As long as he remains with her, she works her distorted will upon him. This is particularly true when he is poised before a moral choice; when he sees clearly in the light of his Cambridge values the correct path for him but hears, with equal clarity, Sawston's voice commanding him to go in an opposite direction. At such moments, Agnes assumes the role of bully previously played by Gerald. However, she will not do so without exposing herself to irony, and the irony is skillful preparation on Forster's part for her final defeat.

Visiting his aunt, Mrs. Failing, in Wiltshire, Rickie learns that Stephen Wonham is his half brother. For Rickie, the discovery is a symbolic moment. To be consummated, it must be shared with Stephen. But Agnes blocks Rickie's intention to do so and later says, "What you call the 'symbolic moment' is over. . . . You tried to tell him. I interrupted you. It's not your fault. You did all you could" (*p.* 158).

Agnes's "reasonableness" makes it difficult to assess fully her tone, but the problem does not alter the fact that she has bullied Rickie and has revealed herself indifferent to symbolic moments, or unable to comprehend them. In this inadequacy lies the irony. Forster tells us elsewhere that she had truly loved Gerald. When Gerald dies, Rickie saves her by making her see, to the best of her ability, that her love and engagement had been a symbolic moment. But this truth could not impress itself permanently upon her. In addition, married to Rickie, she has different needs, and they express themselves in part by a vague contempt, indifference, or ignorance of Rickie's preoccupation with symbolic moments. As a result, she obliviously desecrates the best moment, or period, in her own life: her only experience of authentic love—with Gerald. The irony is one of Forster's deftest touches.

When all has been said about the evil in Agnes and Herbert, and the weakness in Rickie, there remains a need to explain Rickie's involvement in Sawston: in a place and with people antithetical to Cambridge and his college friends.

The cause is, simply, error. We have noted already Rickie's error in making symbols out of people. This mistake prompted him to fall in love with an Agnes of his own creation. He commits a second error: he views marriage itself in a distorted manner. Two years before his engagement he had been warned—appropriately, for him, through the realities disclosed by poetry—to regard marriage properly. He had cherished a passage in Shelley's *Epipsychidion*.

> *I never was attached to that great sect*
> *Whose doctrine is that each one should select*
> *Out of the world a mistress or a friend,*
> *And all the rest, though fair and wise, commend*
> *To cold oblivion,—though it is the code*
> *Of modern morals, and the beaten road*
> *Which those poor slaves with weary footsteps tread*
> *Who travel to their home among the dead*
> *By the broad highway of the world, and so*
> *With one sad friend, perhaps a jealous foe,*
> *The dreariest and the longest journey go.*

Engaged to Agnes, Rickie rejects the message of the poem. His error abets Agnes; it stifles his own impulse to act in opposition to her at moments of moral choice. It does not, however, prevent him from continuing to see, if passively, his own kind of reality. Once married, the truth of what he has done becomes apparent to him. "His wedding had been no mighty landmark . . . love had shown him its infinities already. Neither by marriage nor by any other device can men insure themselves a vision; and Rickie's had been granted him three years before, when he had seen his wife and a dead man clasped in each other's arms. She was never to be so real to him again" (*p.* 189).

It remains for Stephen and Ansell to save Rickie from the domestic quagmire into which he has sunk. Ironically, or more precisely through the meaning of plot, Stephen comes to Rickie through the machinations of Agnes. Rickie's aunt, Mrs. Failing, and her husband had always provided for Stephen. But the widowed Mrs. Failing's interest in Stephen is perilously dependent on her egotism. She needs only the prod of a libelous letter from Agnes to throw Stephen out of her home and to toss after him the papers containing the secret of his relation to Rickie. Stephen reads enough in them to learn that he and Rickie are half brothers. Unaware that Rickie already knows this much and has apathetically collaborated with Agnes to suppress the fact, Stephen travels to Sawston, believing that Rickie will be as pleased to learn that he has a brother as Stephen himself is.

Ansell, too, has gone to see Rickie. Having sent his card in, he sits in the garden of Dunwood House, waiting to be asked in. He is reading a book, "the Essays of Anthony Eustace Failing," and as he reads he twice ignores a greeting—"Morning!"—from Stephen, who has also entered the garden.

Through Forster's own poetic technique, the words Ansell reads prepare him for the eventual acknowledgment of Stephen, still a stranger. When Stephen greets him for a third time, Ansell commends himself to the book. "Very notable was [Mr. Failing's] distinction between coarseness and vulgarity (coarseness, revealing something; vulgarity, concealing something), and his avowed preference for coarseness. Vulgarity, to him, had been the primal curse, the shoddy reticence that prevents man opening his heart to man . . . From it sprang all the things that he hated—class shibboleths, ladies, lidies, the game laws, the Conservative party—all the things that accent the divergencies rather than the similarities in human nature" (*p.* 234).

Mr. Failing's preference for the "similarities in human

nature" is, in fact, too unqualified for an intelligence like
Ansell's. But the distinction between coarseness and vulgarity is appropriate to the moment in the story. Stephen
is coarse; Agnes and Herbert are vulgar. Ansell reads on,
" 'Attain the practical through the unpractical. There is
no other road.' Ansell was inclined to think that the
unpractical is its own reward, but he respected those who
attempted to journey beyond it" (p. 234). Mr. Failing's
words operate in a manner similar to the energizing force
of Forster's own aphorisms, in *Where Angels Fear to
Tread*. The essays in the book Ansell is reading establish
one of the grounds for a spiritual union among himself,
Stephen, and Rickie, all having something of the unpractical in them.

But the immediate relevance of the words Ansell reads
is that they are a symbolic preparation—and we are reminded that "things," like books, can be legitimately employed as symbols—for the meeting between Ansell and
Stephen. A fourth time Stephen greets Ansell, " 'Nice
morning!' " Forster deftly employs the slight alteration, the
judgment that the morning is "nice," to rouse the essential Ansell. "It was not a nice morning, so Ansell felt
bound to speak. He answered: 'No. Why?' A clod of earth
immediately struck him on the back" (p. 234). Ansell
flings Mr. Failing's book at Stephen. They fight. Stephen
is the victor. But the fight, a step forward in their emerging friendship, is also the initial meeting of Cambridge
and Wiltshire.

Ansell and Stephen collaborate, in this scene, to disclose
Stephen's great virtue: he has identity. When Ansell asks
Stephen who he is, his answer gets no further than the
word "I." It is, in context, an excellent reply. Stephen has
no memory of his parents and knows only that he exists.
Such knowledge is denied to many characters in the novel.

Part II, "Sawston," hurries to its climax. Ansell reads the
papers Stephen carries with him and learns the full truth:
Stephen is the son of Rickie's mother. Rickie, Agnes, and
Herbert have simply assumed that Mr. Elliot was the
common parent.

The parlormaid appears to announce that Mrs. Elliot will see Stephen. Surprised that it is not Rickie who invites him in, he enters to be confronted by Agnes. She is convinced that he has come to extort money in exchange for keeping silent about the fact that he and Rickie are half brothers. When the meaning of Agnes's ideas and behavior dawns on Stephen, he leaves, with disgust and contempt. Ansell is then ushered into the house and invited to join "all of us" at dinner, in the boys' dining hall. Ignorant of what has happened, he accepts the invitation, expecting to find Stephen already seated among the rest. Discovering his mistake, he roughly interrogates Rickie within earshot of all the boys.

Recognizing an enemy, Agnes and Herbert order Ansell to leave. Instead—since this is no time for conventional or cultivated behavior—he declaims against the lies and machinations that would victimize Stephen if he were capable of suffering under human assault.

Finally, Rickie bitterly remonstrates with Ansell. "I cannot help my father's disgrace, on the one hand; nor, on the other, will I have anything to do with his blackguard of a son" (p. 254). Previously, Ansell had declared that when the time came he would "hit out like any ploughboy" (p. 204). His simile foreshadows his eventual link with Stephen, although Ansell is most effective when fighting with words and Stephen is often inarticulate. But provoked by Rickie, Ansell delivers his ploughboy's blow. "Please correct two slight mistakes: firstly, Stephen is one of the greatest people I have ever met; secondly, he's not your father's son. He's the son of your mother." Forster adds, "It was Rickie, not Ansell, who was carried from the hall" (p. 255).

There is a certain weakness here. Plot has precipitously dominated characterization. Realistically, it is too early for Ansell to recognize Stephen as "great," but since Forster has conceived Stephen as heroic, he is intent on hastening Ansell to a similar judgment. However, Ansell's exposure of Rickie's and Stephen's true relationship is dramatic and occurs at the right moment in the novel.

Part III, "Wiltshire," begins with a flashback recounting

the circumstances of Stephen's birth. Technically and in context, the device is effective. It has moral meaning. In this flashback "Forster, who so often kills off his living characters, brings to life his dead ones, so that Mr. and Mrs. Elliot reach out from beyond the grave." [11] Forster brings them back realistically and therefore morally, in contrast to Rickie's counterfeit effort to keep his mother alive.

Forster also brings back Robert (Stephen's father), whose last name we recall is never mentioned. By omitting it, Forster not only associates Robert with the prehistoric Britons but displays a skill in plot weaving sometimes absent in the novel. Robert's anonymity reinforces Stephen's feeling of being without forebears. In addition, Robert is a Holy Ghost, whose chief purposes in the novel are to revive Mrs. Elliot's capacity for love, to present her the gift of an "eternal moment," and to father Stephen.

Mr. Failing, already introduced through the essays Ansell has read, also returns in the flashback to play an important role in the plot. He unintentionally brings together Robert and Mrs. Elliot.

When Robert meets Mrs. Elliot at Cadover House, the Failings' house in Wiltshire, he speaks to her of the earth. "He knew when the earth was ill. He knew, too, when she was hungry: he spoke of her tantrums—the strange unscientific element in her that will baffle the scientist to the end of time. . . . As he talked, the earth became a living being—or rather a being with a living skin,—and manure no longer dirty stuff, but a symbol of regeneration and the birth of life from life" (*p. 258*).

Through Robert, Forster has introduced the proper attitude toward the earth, an advance beyond Wordsworth that is nevertheless rooted in the Romantic poet's sensibility and creed. Earth is respected, as much as loved, in *The Longest Journey*; but it is not stable, radiating peace and calm, as parts of it, like stones, rocks, and mountains, are in Wordsworth's poems. The difference is to a degree attributable to one of Forster's persistent themes, "place." Wiltshire is not the Lake country.

But history has more to do with the distinction. Although Forster, like Wordsworth, distrusts the city, he can no longer make the sharp dichotomy between the city and the earth that Wordsworth believed he could. For Forster, the issue is less provincial, and he introduces into the love of the earth a warning against her capriciousness. It is also a warning against too simple a trust in the entire universe.

Love between Robert and Mrs. Elliot follows quickly. When Mr. Elliot, the quintessential man of the city, perversely drives them into each other's arms, they leave for Stockholm. Stephen is conceived there, but his parents' idyll becomes another symbolic moment. After seventeen days, Robert drowns.

Mrs. Elliot contrasts with Agnes. Both loved and both were forced by the death of a loved one to cherish a moment as a completed experience, infinitesmal in the stream of daily life but eternal in the on-going process of the universe. The difference between Mrs. Elliot and Agnes parallels Rickie's ability to perceive the symbolic moment as truth and his erroneous, fateful propensity to turn people into symbols.

The first permits life to continue, both as an uninterrupted process and as one historically punctuated by other symbolic moments. The second fixes the individual in the past. Thus, after Gerald's death, Agnes cannot love again but is immoral and unimaginative enough to marry. Mrs. Elliot, who understands the truth of the symbolic moment, can love again. At first, her affection embraces only Stephen. Then, through love of him, her love for Rickie reawakens. Like the earth itself, the symbolic moment, properly experienced, gives life to the future that comes after it.

The flashback concludes, and the sequential line of the story resumes. Wiltshire, already threaded into Cambridge and Sawston, intensifies and receives the final focus and accent.

The rhythmic recurrence of certain symbolic objects, like the picture of Stockholm, has been discussed here. The over-all structure of the novel has been viewed by K.

W. Gransden as a musical device, a "symphonic three–movement pattern of statement, crisis and resolution, represented by Cambridge, Sawston, and Wiltshire." [12] Clearly, Forster intended the pattern. However, the "resolution" is not simple or obvious. Some have argued that it does not really take place. The truth, like most answers to critical questions, is partial, and will require a close look at the novel's conclusion.

The first important episode after the flashback is an attempted reconciliation between Rickie and Stephen. Stephen returns to Dunwood House, drunk, determined to smash up the place. He "wrecked the hall, lurched up the stairs, fell against the bannisters, balanced for a moment on his spine, and slid over. Herbert called for the police. Rickie, who was upon the landing, caught the man by the knees and saved his life" (p. 275). The act is also Rickie's opportunity for salvation. For the moment, he accepts the choice. He takes command and forces Agnes and Herbert to acquiesce to Stephen's staying. Stephen is put to bed.

But even as Rickie acts heroically and morally, he persists in undermining himself. His pleasure in Stephen's return is really something else: The "son of his mother had come back, to forgive him, as she would have done, to live with him, as she had planned" (p. 276). As Herbert and Rickie carry the drunken Stephen to bed, Forster reiterates Rickie's persistent error: to Rickie, Stephen seems "a symbol of redemption," and like Herbert, he doesn't acknowledge that Stephen is "a man, who would answer . . . back after a few hours' rest" (p. 276).

Rickie does see, for the first time, that he should not have begun the longest journey in the sole company of Agnes. He doesn't see that his journey has always included a ghostly third member, his warped image of his mother.

Stephen attempts to coax Rickie into a complete return to the world of the living; to begin afresh, and properly, the longest journey. Rickie seems responsive and grateful, but offering his hand in brotherhood, gives himself away. Perceiving Rickie's motive, Stephen cries out, " 'I see your game. You don't care . . . to shake *my* hand. . . . You talk to me, but all the time you look at the photograph.' He snatched it up. 'I've my own ideas of good manners. . . .' He tore the photograph across . . . he tore it again. . . . He flung the pieces at the man, who had sunk into a chair" (*p. 283*).

The central object that should not have been turned into a symbol has been destroyed, and Rickie is briefly liberated. For a moment, he sees the truth again. Ironically or tragically, however, his momentary glimpse of it does not revive the ability to act that he had demonstrated when he had saved the drunken Stephen from falling and had then turned on the Pembrokes. His decisiveness had drawn in part upon a falsification of Stephen. No longer able to commit the error, Rickie is drained of his spurious vitality.

But if the truth cannot really "save" Rickie, it can, like Forster's aphorisms, advance the novel's theme, energize the plot, and shift its direction. For the fabric of the story there is substance when Forster depicts a passive but awakened Rickie. "Then [he] was heroic no longer. . . . The man was right. He did not love him, even as he had never hated him. In either passion he had degraded him to be a symbol for the vanished past. . . . Ah, if he had seized those high opportunities! [In Wiltshire, early in the novel, when he had learnt that Stephen was his half brother.] For they led to the highest of all, the symbolic moment, which, if a man accepts, he has accepted life" (*pp. 283–84*).

This return of true perception is a subtle prelude to new action, and as such is a moral implication. Even memory of an occasion for a "symbolic moment," so long as the memory is clear and accurate, endows the moment with the energy to begin a course of activity. At this juncture, it is Stephen who seems intuitively to sense the connection. After Rickie's silent but accurate reverie, Stephen sees that it is really Rickie who needs help, and he ends their quarrel. He offers to take care of him. Although Rickie's moment of true perception is gone and he has slipped back into his old error—he now hears in Stephen's voice the voice of their mother—he does accompany his brother away from Dunwood House. The reunion of the two men, unequal companionship though it is, moves the novel forward.

Another man capable of acting, Ansell, aids the process. He takes Rickie and Stephen into his parents' home. It is, however, only a way station. Rickie and Stephen return to Wiltshire—Rickie to visit Mrs. Failing, Stephen to see the land again. Rickie, still discovering his mother in Stephen, extorts from him a promise not to get drunk. He breaks it. Trivial on its face, Stephen's ensuing alcoholic spree crushes Rickie, who regards it not only as a desecration of their mother but as proof that he had been wrong to trust the earth. (Mrs. Failing had warned him not to.) Searching for the drunken Stephen, Rickie says to the servant who has accompanied him, "Gone bankrupt, Leighton, for the second time. Pretended again that people were real" (*p. 311*). The truth of course is that for the second time he has failed to see that Stephen *is* real.

His perverse, invented burden is too much for Rickie. He comes upon Stephen, lying drunk across the railroad tracks. "Wearily [Rickie] did a man's duty. There was time to raise [Stephen] up and push him into safety. It is also a man's duty to save his own life, and therefore he tried. The train went over his knees. He died up in Cadover, whispering, 'You have been right,' to Mrs. Failing" (*p. 312*).

Rickie's attitude toward the earth, the manner of his death, and the final characterization of Stephen intertwine. Rickie, in his distrust of the earth, sees that Stephen's drunkenness has something to do with the earth. His perception associates in the novel with another symbolic object—a picture of Demeter that had hung in Stephen's room at Cadover house. The story of Demeter, the earth goddess, is the Greek myth for both life and sorrow, a fact recalling one of Mr. Failing's remarks, "Perhaps the earth will neglect our love. Perhaps she will confirm it . . ." (*p. 303*).

Whichever earth does, Forster, or the novel, indicates that we must, without sentimentality, remain close to her, accepting the risks even as we hope for joy. Rickie does attempt to approach the earth courageously, but his nemesis undermines him. The unrectified image of his mother obfuscates to the end of his life his imaginative powers. When the viewpoint is Forster's rather than Rickie's, Mrs. Elliot invokes the myth of Demeter. Rickie, however, clings to an image of his mother that obscures the resemblance. He never fully faces Mrs. Elliot's defiance of society, her sorrow, her passionate self-abandonment in Stockholm to Robert. Perhaps, too, he never fully accepts the fact that she gave birth to Stephen. Forster associates Stephen's intimacy with the earth with his desire to abandon himself in drunkenness. Uniquely equipped to see the truth in myth, Rickie might have remembered that the Greeks regarded Dionysus and Demeter as equally man's greatest friends. He might have lived.

Stephen's relationship to Demeter and Dionysus is, however, more complex than it seems at first. The question is, how does his connection with them help characterize him, especially towards the end of the novel?

Leaving aside for the moment his mythic associations, two processes, both begun early in the novel, focus together at the conclusion to emphasize Stephen's essence. One is the train of events that make actual the idea of Stephen as hero. The other is the creation of an unusual dimension in him—the relation of his being to time.

Demeter and Dionysus contribute only to Stephen's heroic image. They are not connected with the time dimension that contributes to his characterization. And even the influence of these deities upon the affirmation of Stephen as hero is mixed.

Stephen as hero has been adumbrated throughout the novel. Mrs. Failing, superciliously referring to him as one, speaks more truth than she knows. Ansell has precipitously called him "great." Rickie, even when finally wearied by his own illusions, describes Stephen as a "law to himself" (p. 311). Pertinent also is a fact extraneous to the novel as we have it; Forster once thought of naming him "Siegfried." [13]

Demeter, however, who so often supports the suggestion of his heroism, steps aside during Stephen's last drunken and perilous spree and refuses for the duration of this episode to cooperate in the process leading toward his conclusive emergence as hero. There is no contradiction here. We have been told that Demeter, or the earth, might neglect our love. But her refusal to protect her devotee at so critical a time almost cancels his apotheosis as hero. Only later, when Stephen is married and the father of a daughter, is Demeter's presence again felt.

It would seem that her withdrawal during the episode when Stephen's life is in danger is to give Dionysus the opportunity to amplify Stephen's heroism. But even this hypothesis is flawed, if not altogether untrue. To an extent, Stephen's recklessness is Dionysian. However, to be crushed under the wheels of a train is thin in ultimate meaning, even Dionysian. Moreover, Stephen does live: he is not finally a victim of Dionysian frenzy. His survival is an evasion of the meaning of the myth. The true Dionysian hero is heroic because he dies as a sacrifice to the god's power, and thus answers the question whether it is better to live a long placid life or a short one intensified by adherence to the Dionysian experience. The mythic moral meaning is roughly analogous to the choice that confronted Achylleus.

What does happen in the novel is that Rickie, who has written stories about getting close to nature and who might have been a follower of Demeter, is accepted by Dionysus as a substitute sacrifice for Stephen. But this is either brilliantly subtle or too subtle. The second possibility arises because Rickie's heroism remains dubious, while Stephen's becomes established as a definitive fact.

However, the other characteristic that attends Stephen's final substantiation—his relationship to time—is treated by Forster with a firm hand, possibly because only Demeter and not Dionysus is in attendance. Whatever the reason, Forster in this matter is guided by an imaginative cogency resembling Rickie's at its best.

Again, the time dimension of Stephen has been anticipated throughout the novel. Relatively early, we are told that he "worried infinity as if it was a bone" (*p. 104*).

Near the beginning of Part III, "Wiltshire," he loses his sense of identity when he is out of doors at night—when he is closest to Demeter.

But it is at the novel's conclusion that the definitive evidence is given. Once more, Demeter is a presence, and this time she cooperates to bring into single focus Stephen's heroism and the time dimension that expands the characterization of him.

Married and the father of a girl, Stephen takes the child to sleep with him out of doors one night when Ansell is visiting. Ansell remains in the house with Stephen's wife, a truly shadowy and undeveloped figure, as befits the wife, Forster implies, of a mythic hero.

Lying in the open with his daughter clutching his hand, Stephen reflects and wonders, "He was alive and had created life. By whose authority? Though he could not phrase it, he believed that he guided the future of our race, and that, century after century, his thoughts and his passions would triumph in England. The dead who had evoked him, the unborn whom he would evoke—he governed the paths between them. By whose authority?" (*p.* 320).

These thoughts and much else in the novel contrast with the comparative weightlessness of England in *Where Angels Fear to Tread*. Not only Cambridge, the quasi-mystical aura of many of the Wiltshire scenes, and Stephen's metaphysical speculations about himself as an infinite hero of England, but the elaborate treatment of the same Sawston that figured in the first novel give England its proper density of detail, tradition, and strength.

More to the point, however, is that the association of Stephen with time—past, present, and future—places a new accent on his heroism. Unlike the other characters, he is in the present but not imprisoned by it. His metaphysical time dimension not only liberates him from conventional realism, even as the latter is represented by Ansell, but gives him both the flexibility to act in the world he has been born into and a sense of historical proportion about the brief span he will actually spend in that world. This sense is denied to the other characters, and therefore

Stephen has a superior instinctive wisdom in his personal relations with them. Forster has once again emphasized his affinity with his mythic intimates, Demeter and Dionysus, themselves infinite and timeless in meaning.

Forster's propensity for introducing into a subsequent novel, in a new and modified form, a theme previously treated, is also pertinent. In *A Room with a View*, a central character will live in the present but not be defined by it. However, this character will have no metaphysical sense of the past, and his heroism will depend, among other differences, on his eloquence, a faculty logically denied to Stephen.

One more figure, Ansell, remains to be discussed. Although he all but fades from the last pages, the fact is not a technical weakness. It is enough that his friendship with Stephen is suggested.

Rickie was the mediating influence in the creation of this friendship, and his effectiveness is an unequivocal assertion of his salvation, distinct from the ambivalent implications of his sacrifice. However, the impossibility of discussing Ansell without returning to Rickie and Stephen indicates that Forster intended poetic as well as intellectual Cambridge to unite at the end. The intention is plausible, within the context of the novel, but would have been so difficult to achieve that Forster was wise in leaving it suggestive, through the sketchy presence of Ansell alone at night with Stephen's wife.

More open to the possibility of convincing development is the union of poetic Cambridge, as represented by Rickie, already Hellenistic in imagination and the author of stories about getting in touch with the earth; with mythic Wiltshire, also enriched by the symbolic presence and activities of Greek deities. Rickie has left Stephen a legacy at once poetic and material—the stories Rickie has written. They are publishable and will bring Stephen money. Possible, too, is John Beer's conclusion, ". . . thanks to Rickie, imagination has supervened to transfigure [Stephen's] mortal clay and bring him into complete reconciliation with the universe." [14]

The form taken by Stephen's gratitude for Rickie's

material and spiritual gifts is an excellent addition to the characterization of Stephen. He gently corrects Rickie, and thus exhibits the wisdom and ability to make wise decisions that are aspects of his completed emergence as a hero. Rickie tried, by inaccurately turning his dead mother into a symbol, to keep her alive. Stephen, with a more accurate sense of possibility, and suggesting, incidentally, that his mysticism does not preclude an instinct for the realism of immediacy, fulfills Rickie's hope for Mrs. Elliot's immortality by naming his own daughter after her. "Stephen . . . and these are the last words of the novel '. . . had given [his daughter] the name of their mother.' The word 'their' is the significant one: Rickie lives on . . . the brothers are united at last, and through the body; and Mrs. Elliot's bid for life is justified." [15]

Nevertheless, with respect to Rickie alone a question remains. He was in error to the end of his life and died with the wrong words on his lips. Furthermore, his gifts from "beyond the grave" deserve gratitude but do not oblige Stephen, who in fact does not, to sentimentalize over Rickie's mistakes and weakness. His only justification, the sole reason for complying with the suggestion that his action, in saving Stephen, though he was too weary to save himself, is faintly heroic—and more emphatically so in its consequences—is that in death he has been purified into his own imagination at its best. He *is*, finally, the stories and perhaps a transfiguring spiritual influence bequeathed to Stephen. Unanswered, however, is whether the poetic imagination, even at its best and perceptive of truths unavailable to other human faculties, can either effectively oppose or live in the same world with what is "thick, and lasts."

Flawed in some ways, successful in others, *The Longest Journey* is another turning point for Forster. Fantasy and romance have given way, as windows upon the truth, to a concept of the poetic imagination more fully explored than the former idea, romance, had been. They have been replaced, too, by the morally fortified intellect and the instinctual life of the blood. England has been given the substance and tradition in depth she lacked in *Where Angels Fear to Tread*. The unanswerable questions about infinity have been asked and although answered as a technique in the characterization of Stephen, have, as general metaphysical problems, sensibly remained unanswered.

Forster has enlarged his vision. As a consequence, he returns to his second "Italian novel" — *A Room with a View*, begun before *The Longest Journey* but put aside. His return to *A Room with a View* suggests that writing *The Longest Journey* had a liberating effect, although the exact relation and process is not clear. Nevertheless, some continuity is apparent. *The Longest Journey* was, for Forster, in addition of course to an achievement in its own right and terms, a pause in the act of resolving the problems of *Where Angels Fear to Tread* and simultaneously taking up new themes. As to the latter, they will best be considered in a discussion devoted entirely to *A Room with a View*. But the unresolved problems of *Where Angels Fear to Tread* can be reviewed here by way of anticipation. Social comedy, discernable among the threads of *Where Angels Fear to Tread* and not heretofore alluded to in this study, was handled brilliantly but fundamentally simply and without extraordinary subtlety in its relation to the other strands making up the novel's pattern. Sexuality, already discussed, was not only unsuccessfully introduced and pursued but never really reconciled with either romance or Forster's most fundamental creed, embracing all others — humanism. In *A Room with a View*, he was freed, for whatever reasons, to work social comedy into a truly subtle device, undergoing transformation as the novel proceeds, appearing at times as technique, at others, as theme. He faced again, and this time with success, the theme of sexuality. The result is that *A Room with a View* is Forster's first, and perhaps only, novel about a happy, consummated relationship between a man and a woman.

SOCIAL COMEDY, a light occasionally reaching incandescence within A *Room with a View*, joins with Forster's attempt to create a realistic love between a man and a woman. The effort to guide matters in such a way that the union between the lovers arises convincingly out of circumstances requires Forster, however, to guard and check the social comedy.

He is compelled to do so because the comedy, though joined with the love affair, does not have the same significance as the latter. Love between a man and a woman, culminating in a happy marriage, is, whatever else it may be, Forster's effort to extend the bounds of his private view of humanism. In what is essentially for Forster an experiment, he is disinclined to give social comedy an arch and continuous emphasis.

It would seem that he had become intellectually and emotionally convinced that his own humanism must widen its scope to include heterosexual love but, unsure of his temperamental and experiential ability to convert the theme into character and event, he was unwilling to give to so dangerous an imp as social comedy a license and continuous force, lest it interfere with his experiment. Nevertheless, always the resourceful artist, he not only turns his restrictions upon comedy into subtle and effective technical devices. He masks their primary purpose and causes these restrictions to serve other ends.

A somewhat less biographical and more historical explanation of Forster's attempt, in A *Room with a View*, to widen humanism—to be cautious in the process about giving social comedy its head, is that he began the novel in 1903 but did not finish it until 1908. In the interval, pessimism about humanism's relevance to contemporary problems had become increasingly persuasive. Forster, independent in this respect, refused to acknowledge pessimism as intellectually mandatory.

But he knew, and had even experienced, the reasons for its claims. His affirmation of humanism in A *Room with a View* was therefore necessarily defensive; his posture, as author, limited his laughter. But his skill—avoidance of stridency and achieving a tone of casual ease—mutes his defensiveness. The latter limits the range of comedy but remains historical and biographical. It never appears in the texture, mood, or theme of the novel.

Rather, we are more conscious of technical daring. Forster's characteristic non-Aristotelian attitude toward plot [1] is again in evidence. But this time Forster has gone further. In defiance of Aristotle's dictum, he permits character—embodied in one of the protagonists (Mr. Emerson, a vigorous old humanist)—to generate plot. Here, Forster gives to character a degree of control unusual even among his own novels.

The technical risk-taking is successful and achieves the goal towards which Forster's interest in technique is always deliberately or implicitly directed: the expression, through structural inventiveness, of moral meaning. The most obvious result in A *Room with a View* is that control of plot by character expresses one of the novel's major concerns: the responsibility of the individual to be heroic—to accept a moral imperative to defy society and consequently influence, shape, or control its future.

Finally, Forster links, through what is almost sleight of hand, a theme of the novel—love—with two technical aspects—comedy and the power of character to generate plot. In doing so, he does not use comedy and character to express love (the theme). Rather—and with intriguing results—he transforms love into a third element of technique. As love becomes, like comedy and the function of character, a structural device, it enters into an amoral intrigue. It joins with comedy to support character's successful bid for power over plot.

But if love, a theme, is transformed into a technique, the reverse process occurs in Forster's treatment of a primarily technical aspect—the comic. It becomes a theme, or more specifically, an inherent part of character and a determinant of the relationship between character and society, although that relationship is conceived, by Forster, in a fresh manner. "A Room with a View," F. C. Crews notes, ". . . is a philosophical novel; and . . . gives an unorthodox twist to the traditional comedy of manners. In most works of this genre the humor derives from the failure of certain characters to fulfill their social roles, whereas here the comic characters are . . . those who take society too seriously. The only ones who survive Forster's . . . barbs are those whose 'view' enables them to see through the social code and recognize their enduring relationships to nature and their fellow men." [2]

This summary generalization, accurate enough, does not, however, suggest the subtlety of Forster's use of comedy in characterization. Mr. Emerson, who has already been described here as an energetic, elderly humanist, is not only one of the chief protagonists. He is not only the character who more than any of the others, shapes, directs, and controls the plot. He is also a triumphant result of Forster's use of comedy as an active, changing process for the purpose of characterization. Mr. Emerson begins as an apparently comic figure. He concludes as anything but comic—as the most powerful figure in the novel. He not only does not take society seriously, which means that he seriously rejects many of its values; he indirectly influences society's future. We recall that this is precisely the moral result of the technical fact, an impossibility had he remained comic, that he controls the plot.

His power also derives from an historical dimension Forster gives him. He is reminiscent of the early Carlyle, of the party of humanity—really a religious sect, and of Samuel Butler.

His association with Butler is the most explicit, though curiously not the most convincing. Lee Holt, noting that Forster, during the years of A *Room with a View*'s composition, intended to write a study of Butler, calls attention to Mr. Emerson's paraphrasing of Butler and referring to him as "a friend of mine." [3] However, when one thinks of the differences between Mr. Emerson and the historical Butler, the impulse to speculate upon why Forster was able to create Mr. Emerson but unable to complete a biography of Butler grows strong. Butler's humanism, unlike Mr. Emerson's, lacked Forster's own new faith in love between men and women.

Part I of the novel is set in Florence. At the Pension Bertolini, Mr. Emerson, overhearing that an English girl, Lucy Honeychurch, and her cousin-chaperone, Charlotte Bartlett, lack a "view" of the Arno, booms out a generous offer to give up to the ladies the rooms occupied by himself and his son, George, a melancholy and passive young man. Through his impulsive generosity, Mr. Emerson shocks and alienates Charlotte, who is, like himself, potentially a lifelong comic figure at this point. (It is interesting that both will play noncomic roles in Part II, though Charlotte will do so in a shadowy and ambivalent manner.)

At the Pension Bertolini we also meet Mr. Beebe, an English clergyman on tour. He is contrapuntal to Charlotte, seemingly attractive at first but growing increasingly unpleasant toward the novel's conclusion. In Part I, however, he is at his best, and one of his more important roles is to explain Mr. Emerson to the cousins, "He has the merit—if it is one—of saying exactly what he means." And referring to Mr. Emerson's offer to exchange rooms, Mr. Beebe continues, "He no more thought of putting you under an obligation than he thought of being polite. It is so difficult . . . to understand people who speak the truth. . . . He has no tact and no manners . . . and he will not keep his opinions to himself" (*pp.* 15–16).

These insights are accurate enough, but just as Mr. Beebe himself will prove limited, his understanding of Mr. Emerson is confined to the implications of the latter's social behavior. For a fuller grasp of Mr. Emerson, we must note his words, his actions, his son George's dutiful quoting of him, and Lucy Honeychurch's response to these.

Like Forster, Mr. Emerson selects and emphasizes the aspects of humanism most relevant to the early twentieth century, or seemingly both most sophisticated and most enduring at that period. The early Carlyle said "yes" to work, and George Meredith and the party of humanity said yes to sexuality, but in a discreet and muffled Victorian voice. Mr. Emerson carries on the creed of the latter, but he gives an openness, boldness, and directness to their message that they themselves did not always achieve. Speaking to Lucy, he echoes Meredith, but manages to sound more radical than his source.[4] "Do you suppose there's any difference between spring in nature and spring in man? But there we go, praising the one and condemning the other as improper, ashamed that the same laws work eternally through both" (*pp. 80–81*).

Moreover, his faith in love is grounded in a kind of existentialism that has always been the logical conclusion of the humanist tradition. He quotes A. E. Housman.

> *From far, from eve and morning,*
> *And you twelve-winded sky,*
> *The stuff of life to knit me*
> *Blew hither: here am I.*

He adds, "George and I . . . know that we come from the winds, and that we shall return to them; that all life is perhaps a knot, a tangle, a blemish in the eternal smoothness. But why should this make us unhappy? Let us rather love one another, and . . . rejoice" (*p. 38*).

In Forster's first two published novels, particularly in *Where Angels Fear to Tread*, aphorisms energize events following them. In *A Room with a View*, however, although aphorisms are again used frequently, they no longer have the unique function they enjoyed in the earlier novels. They have become generalized with other evidence of Mr. Emerson's eloquence, and as the conclusion

of the novel makes clear, his eloquence—in whatever manifestation—is significant.

Nevertheless, Mr. Emerson's aphorisms elaborate his
creed and thus amplify Forster's characterization of him.
In one, which he delivers in conversation with Lucy, he
reveals his prophetic impulse. But the main emphasis is
again sexuality, "The Garden of Eden . . . which you
place in the past, is really yet to come. We shall enter it
when we no longer despise our bodies" (*pp. 154–55*).

A Room with a View, Lionel Trilling has said, "deals
with the physical reality upon which all the other realities
rest. The blindness to this reality is the source of the
comedy . . . played out to the verge of tragedy." [5] Mr.
Emerson's roots in the party—or religion—of humanity,
his traditional existentialism, his aphoristic faith that man
will someday become again more natural, are of course
evidence that he is not blind to physical reality. This
evidence also reaffirms that he begins as a potential comic
butt but does not remain one. Rather, if the blindness of
others is the true comic aspect of the novel, and if the
comedy they create carries the story to the verge of tragedy—a loveless marriage—he will prevent the principal
blinded character—Lucy Honeychurch—from going over
the edge.

Today, Mr. Emerson's sexual creed does not seem particularly profound, or other than tame. But in *A Room with
a View* it is technically effective. It establishes a position
from which others can be judged, explained, opposed, or
helped. Mr. Emerson's faith in physical reality, part of the
substance of his presence, operates as one of the determi-
nants of the plot structure.

One reason that this is so is that Mr. Emerson is, like
Stephen Wonham, not quite of the time and place inhab-
ited by the characters around him. But unlike Stephen, he
is not mythic and primordial. He is a Victorian and a
prophet of the early twentieth-century's future. Like his
historical models, he is in the present but not of it. The
other characters sense this. Seizing upon his alien aspects,
they attempt to expel him from the narrow country of

their own minds. They fail. Despite his larger vision, he is as concerned with the facts of their country as they are.

Quoting to Lucy his father's rhetoric, George amplifies Mr. Emerson's social and historical realism and relevance, "My father . . . says that there is only one perfect view—the view of the sky straight over our heads, and that all these views on earth are but bungled copies of it" (*p. 194*). If we recall that Rickie Elliot's poetic imagination disclosed aspects of reality inaccessible to other human faculties, we realize that George has said that his father urges humanity, not to aspire metaphysically for a realm of Platonic ideas, but to think of an historical future on earth. The "bungled copies" are not imperfect imitations of an Absolute. They are social distortions, produced by time and events, particularly the cumulative force of custom, but still mutable—malleable, for the better—by the same process.

Of incidental interest is the Hellenic derivation of the imagery and the secularization of Plato. The whole process suggests Forster's somewhat uncritical sympathy for G. Lowes Dickenson's attempt to combine Hellenism with social awareness and activity. But because Forster as novelist exercises control over Mr. Emerson, and places him in a context of Forster's own creation, G. Lowes Dickenson's literal attempt to reconcile two interests becomes, in *A Room with a View*, metaphor. As such, as a way of expressing social insight, it is effective. It is not to be assessed by the same standards of effectiveness to which the interests and career of Dickenson must submit. Mr. Emerson's effectiveness is to be judged by his role in relation to the plot and his influence upon the other characters. Since he will be seen, in this light, to be eminently successful, his metaphoric speech becomes endowed with the relevance and reality of his achievement within the novel. It becomes an active expression, in poetry, of social truth.

George tells Lucy about another reference to "views" made by his father. "He [said] . . . that views are really crowds—crowds of trees and houses and hills—and are bound to resemble each other, like human crowds—and that the power they have over us is something supernatural, for the same reason. . . . For a crowd is more than the people who make it up. Something gets added to it . . . just as something has got added to those hills' " (*pp.* 194–95).

As in the other discussion of views—"the bungled copies"—the poetry in this one is political, social, and ethical. The crowd's "supernatural power," in 1908, is human cohesion. It contrasts with the structure and values of Lucy's home, Surrey, which takes for granted its internal connections and excludes both the rest of England and the world itself. What Mr. Emerson, who sees the paradox of the human condition, is saying is that only through human coherence can true individualism be realized.

And it is his own individualism—or difference from others, as suggested by Crews' remark concerning the conventionality and unconventionality distinguishing the characters who play comic roles in the novels from those who do not—that is as much a source of his strength as it is of his alienation. Lucy faintly denies to George that there is anything special about one of Mr. Emerson's particular qualities—his readiness to help others. She insists that we all try to be kind. George replies, "Because we think it improves our characters. But he is kind to people because he loves them; and they find him out, and are offended, or frightened" (*p.* 35).

It will not be a digression to point out that George has also assessed characters in Forster's first two novels. Philip Herriton and Rickie Elliot, even Caroline Abbot, can revere more easily than they can love. George, or Forster, has generalized them into the English middle class and has perceived its generic weakness: a fear of invasion born out of a secret feeling of unworthiness. In *A Room with a View*, however, the problem is to connect this fear with insularity, which is as aggressive as it is fear-ridden. George has done this for us, or rather, Mr. Emerson has, and the latter's characterization has been further enlarged and explored. His active opposition to conventional behavior—to comic blindness that can lead to tragedy—has been anchored in the psychology of personal relations. A prophetic visionary about the political and social future of the "crowd," he is also a hero in the realm of personal relations.

The essential point—and it is fully developed late in the novel—is that for Forster the distinction between personal relations and those customarily called "political" or "social" is meaningless. As "time went on," John Crowe Ransom has written, ". . . it grew upon him that politics . . . scarcely reaches to the heart." [6] Even more relevant is an observation by Forster himself, although it was made in 1957, nearly fifty years after he published A Room with a View. Watching an English girl walking arm-in-arm with Greek girls in a part of their country reputed to be anti-British, he reflected, "Her action . . . is the only sort . . . that can lighten our darkness. Conferences cannot utilise it. . . . They are soused in nationalism. It is only when personal contacts are established that the axis of our sad planet shifts and the stars shine through the ground-fog." [7]

In A Room with a View, "personal contact" means simply love between a man and a woman, specifically, between George and Lucy. Their love will have to be achieved and consummated in defiance of convention and the fear-ridden blindness of Surrey. But in the philosophy and psychology of Forster, the convention and fear that will create obstacles for Lucy and George are the same forces that make political conferences useless. The kindness of Mr. Emerson, the developed heart suggested by Ransom, the spontaneous comaraderie of the English girl and her Greek acquaintances, equate successful personal relations with the political hopes of mankind. Mr. Emerson, near the conclusion of the novel, will make the equation explicit.

Analogously, falling in love with Lucy is for George a return to life itself. When we first meet him, in the early Italian chapters, he suffers from "a deep, neurotic, fin de siècle pessimism." [8] But a sudden confrontation in Florence with death (we are reminded of his father's existentialism) rouses him to love of Lucy and life.

However, in a scene set in Fiesole, reminiscent of Richard Feverel's first meeting with Lucy Desborough, George kisses Lucy Honeychurch and is temporarily cast down again. The reason is not that she rebuffs him. She doesn't. The reason lies in that area where, for Forster, the obstacles to personal relations and the processes of politics are one and the same. The kiss has been observed by Charlotte Bartlett, a voyeur lacking Rickie Elliot's poetic imagination. Charlotte whisks Lucy away to Rome, where she meets a proper Englishman, Cecil Vyse.

Part II is set in England, and the sustained presence of England, if only as suburbia, creates challenges avoided by Forster in his first "Italian" novel, *Where Angels Fear to Tread*. Aided by plot contrivance and the power of character, Surrey not only offers resistance to the temper of Italy—embodied in the buried but still living passional experience of George and Lucy—but through its resistance, as well as its customary daily activities, defines itself. In an ironic reversal of Forster's first novel, England has become the land of "tradition." However insular and insufficient the values of Surrey are, they, like the historical forces that shape the setting—Monteriano—in *Where Angels Fear to Tread*, create the world in which action will occur, individuals will be tested, and universal truths will not only be disclosed but will become the focus and emphasis of the novel's conclusion.

Lucy has become engaged to Cecil Vyse, who quickly reveals himself to be the Willoughby Patterne of this partially Meredithian story. Cecil dislikes Lucy's friends and neighbors. He perceives their provincialism but for the wrong reason—cultural snobbery. And he decides unpleasantly to play upon them what he considers a joke. He recommends for a house-to-let in Lucy's community a father and son whom he has met in a London museum and whom he regards as crude. The prospective tenants, who do take the house, are, of course, Mr. Emerson and George. And an invitation from Lucy's mother brings Charlotte back into the story and onto the scene.

Coincidence and surprise have interlocked Parts I and

ii, Italy and England, and will subserve character as the latter begins to direct not only plot but fate. At first glance, the idea of coincidence or surprise offering itself up to the resourceful character, rather than determining the fate of character, seems whimsical in a novelist as rooted in the Victorian tradition as Forster is. But that tradition itself has been oversimplified. Explaining Forster, K. W. Gransden makes an unexpected but revealing association, "Surprise . . . keeps things continually alive. . . . To be on the side of what Hardy called 'hap' is to be on the side of life." [9] Another way of looking at the matter would be to see that Forster, like Hardy, discovered the roots of early modernism in the only logical place to seek them, Victorianism, but in its full complexity.

George steals a second kiss, different in meaning from the first, since Lucy is now engaged. But in his revived boldness he assures her that Cecil is the wrong man for her and that he himself is the right one. Lucy is startled and frightened by the kiss into her periodic role as one of the comic but dangerous blind, in which she can best support the expectations of Surrey. She rebuffs George. He does, however, effectively influence her. She not only breaks her engagement to Cecil but in explaining her reasons to him, unconsciously uses George's ideas and arguments. Comedy has not only been played out to the verge of tragedy but has, for once, functioned also in the rescue.

The danger, however, is not over. Lucy, still on the side of Surrey, cannot admit to herself that she has been in love with George while engaged to Cecil. She resolves to marry no one and prepares to flee to Greece, ironically the twin fountain, along with Italy, of the fully realized life within the tradition of Western culture. She will be accompanied by two elderly maidens—the Misses Alan—first encountered at the Pension Bertolini, in Part i. They will take the place of Charlotte Bartlett, who is now ready for a very different role. In Greece, they will stop Lucy's eyes and ears, and perhaps whisk her away should passion, in any form, threaten. Lucy is preparing to repeat the tragicomedy of Part i.

But she does not leave. In the episode that convinces her to stay, the transformations of roles so pertinent to the plot of *A Room with a View* are completed. The power of Mr. Emerson to direct the plot emerges in significant action, and Surrey is not only defeated but attains symbolically increased stature through the fact that a species of heroism is required in the battle leading to Surrey's defeat.

Partly as a result of "surprise"—one of the forces of life in the novel, partly through the action of the increasingly enigmatic Charlotte, Lucy encounters Mr. Emerson in the house of Mr. Beebe. The latter, seemingly attractive in the initial scenes in the Pension Bertolini, has by now revealed himself to be the logical, if hypothetical, conclusion to Surrey's denial of the heart. He is against all marriage, the form of personal relations in *A Room with a View* which, when the result of authentic love, will be equated with political and social opposition to Surrey. His presence in the episode, and the defeat of his desire that Lucy *should* go off to Greece with the Misses Alan, will therefore connote more than the frustration of his unpleasant private will.

Moreover, from the point of view of plot and characterization, it is important that the defeat of Surrey takes place in his home. At the Pension Bertolini, when it seemed that Mr. Emerson was to be cast in a comic role, Mr. Beebe was the indulgent, somewhat perceptive—and therefore superior—source of the former's characterization. Because, however, the central scene of Part II, in which Mr. Emerson will defeat Surrey, will be played in the study of Mr. Beebe, who is the symbolic voice of Surrey at its worst, the two men will now exchange roles. And since the field of action will be Mr. Beebe's own house, through an ironic inversion Parts I and II of the plot will be supplied with an additional jointure.

When Lucy unexpectedly meets Mr. Emerson in the study—she is still determined to leave England and he is at first ignorant of her having broken her engagement to Cecil—Mr. Emerson, with characteristic and effective disregard of Edwardian convention, addresses himself to the central theme of the novel, " 'I taught [George] to trust in

love.' I said: 'When love comes, that is reality.' I said:
'Passion does not blind . . . [it] is sanity . . .'" (*p. 240*).

Assigned to a young man, these words would have
sounded callow. But in reserving the speech for Mr. Emerson, Forster accomplishes a number of technical ends. He
realistically represents the felt reminiscence, about love, of
an old man. More important, he incorporates in Mr.
Emerson the lost historical idea that eloquence signified
the presence, not the absence, of truth. As a result, Mr.
Emerson is able, finally, to influence Lucy and thus to
direct the plot and achieve his victory over Surrey.

When Cecil is finally mentioned, Lucy cannot lie,
"Somehow it was impossible to cheat this old man" (*p.
245*). Armed with the new information that she has broken her engagement, Mr. Emerson, wise in the ways of
using power, seizes the strategic moment, "Take an old
man's word," he says, "there is nothing worse than a
muddle. . . . Do you remember . . . when you refused the
room with a view? [That was a muddle]—little, but
ominous—and I am fearing that you are in one now." He
then delivers the home thrust, "You love George! . . .
You won't marry the other man for his sake" (*pp. 246–
47*).

The effect intended by Mr. Emerson is shock. In Lucy,
who, in blinding herself to her love of George, had
"sinned against Eros and Pallas Athene" and had entered
"the vast armies of the benighted" (*p. 214*), awareness
and denial now clash. But Mr. Emerson has subverted her.
She leaves the ranks of those armies, and Mr. Beebe,
who has entered the study, thinking that Lucy has been
saying good-by to Mr. Emerson, preparatory to leaving for
Greece, learns the truth. Cynically—but really admitting
defeat—he advises Lucy to marry George. There is nothing wrong with the boy, Mr. Beebe says, "except that he
no longer interests me. Marry [him], Miss Honeychurch.
He will do admirably" (*p. 249*).

The decision is made. But voices from outside—
muddle and unaware of the view beyond Mr. Beebe's
study which symbolizes Surrey as a place (at its worst)—

call. They are, in urging Lucy to hurry—the Misses Alan
are about to depart for Greece—pressing her to separate
from George. "She turned to Mr. Emerson in despair. But
his face revived her. It was the face of a saint who understood." He says, "If I were George, and gave you one
kiss, it would make you brave. You have to go cold into a
battle that needs warmth. . . . we fight for more than
Love or Pleasure . . . [for] Truth." Lucy replies, " 'You
kiss me. . . . I will try.' He gave her the sense of deities
reconciled, a feeling that, in gaining the man she loved,
she would gain something for the whole world" (*pp.*
249–50).

Mr. Emerson has won—control of the plot and victory
over Surrey. But like all men of power, in his triumph he
has disclosed an additional goal heretofore patiently concealed. When Mr. Emerson says that a kiss from George
would make her brave for "battle," when Lucy asks him to
kiss her in George's significant absence, when she senses
after the kiss that she will gain something for the whole
world, Forster suggests the knighting of a squire about to
do battle for a religious truth. And the religious connotation is simply one more aspect of Forster's central unity—
the existential identity of successful personal relations,
effective political and social action, and, in short, any
conceivable enlargement of humanistic values and aspirations.

The medieval suggestion accompanying Lucy's transformation into a heroine is, however, worth noting as a
technical device in itself. We are told previously, in anticipation of his disclosure as the wrong man, that Cecil is
medieval (*p. 106*)—essentially ascetic. And Forster's own
dislike of the Middle Ages has often been commented
upon.[10] An unsympathetic critic of Forster will therefore
see unintended contradiction in the borrowing of imagery
from the Middle Ages—Forster will do so again, incidentally, in his next novel *Howards End* (1910). But the
better disposed critic will see instinct and skill in the
process.

In the case of Lucy, the most prosaic and realistic fact is

that she has been transformed into a heroine by the voice of the nineteenth-century religion of humanity. Whatever its merits, this religion was impoverished in imagery. Borrowing from a colorful era is therefore essential to Forster's novelistic purpose. A heroine about to battle for love, truth, and the world would not, were she colorless, suit the suggestive mood and tone or the symbolic intention of A Room with a View. The historical roots of Mr. Emerson's philosophy are not the main theme of the story.

This, however, is an elaboration of a secondary, if interesting, technical matter. A more central question is, once Lucy's heroism has been established, its actual essence. The literal fact is that her heroism causes little disturbance. Surrey at its best—that is to say when it is represented by Lucy's family and friends rather than by Mr. Beebe—prides itself on its advanced ideas and will be shocked not by the broken engagement but by the belief that Lucy, while engaged to Cecil, was conscious of loving George and intent on having him. From a literal viewpoint, the conventions of Surrey will be admonished rather than overthrown.

Nevertheless, there is, in Lucy's transformation and action, a real sword thrust into the social fabric. But since Surrey will not even feel the blow—and much less in its continuing protective blindness will it be overwhelmed or thrown into chaos—the deeper essence of Lucy's heroism, within the context of the novel, is hypothetical and symbolic. In defiance of convention, she has opted for the heart. This, the real threat, will not be understood in its full implications by Surrey, complacent in its insularity.

Still to be considered, however, is Lucy's conviction that she will gain something for the whole world. There is the generalized suggestion, typical of all of Forster's political allusions, that most of the world suffers from an inadequately developed heart. Moreover, in 1908, this deficiency could be seen as historically recurrent inertia and as philosophic ignorance. In the novel, both are embodied in Surrey and symbolized by it.

The denial of the needs of the heart, by Surrey and the world at large, has occurred partly through an historical process, but one producing a resolvable dilemma. Regulations governing personal relations are needed and grow in accordance with the development of the other characteristics of a given society. However, this process includes also a resistance to conscious and deliberate change. The result is muddle, an inability to see that change *has* taken place. Only the hero or heroine can see that new values have emerged historically and that the conventions designed to guard the old ones are therefore outdated. In this sense, Lucy's defiance of Edwardian suburbia's conventions is historically symbolic. It is action against a universal paradigm that must always be opposed by heroism.

The philosophic ignorance challenged by Lucy's heroism is unawareness that life being perilous, love ought to be all the more cherished. This truth was made explicit by Lucy's mentor and guide, Mr. Emerson, early in the novel. It was also anticipated by an episode characteristic of Forster—one which recurs, with variations, in all his novels: an accident, or near-accident, to a conveyance, followed by temporary liberation of emotions.

In *Where Angels Fear to Tread,* a carriage overturns, Gino's baby is killed, and Philip Herriton is momentarily roused to manly action. In *The Longest Journey,* the station tram conveying Rickie Elliot from the Cambridge railroad station to his college rooms loses a wheel. He might have been killed, but he laughs—it is the only time that he does—and had he retained the ability to do so he might not have entered the disastrous marriage with Agnes. In *Howards End,* an automobile will collide with a cart and with life itself, again producing temporarily heightened emotion and self-transcendance in a central character. In *A Passage to India* (1924), an automobile will, in the night, hit an unknown animal and the different occupants of the car will be moved, each according to his previous history, to new heights of love or fear.

In *A Room with a View,* the accident occurred on the return from the outing during which George had first kissed Lucy, only to be observed by Charlotte, who, in Italy, was the implacable enemy of the Emersons and of the heart. The English are riding in carriages. Lightning strikes an overhead tramline wire and a support falls. But they stop just in time. "They chose to regard it as a miraculous preservation. . . . they embraced each other. . . . For a moment they realized vast possibilities of good" (*p. 90*).

The "good" is most obviously a Bloomsbury ideal derived from G. E. Moore.[11] It is also, since personal relations and politics are one for Forster, not only an expression of the heart but a moral imperative giving political connotations to the heroine who will act in its behalf. However, "the vast possibilities of good" were realized in a moment of peril, and the hero or heroine sees in this fact another paradigm of the universal human condition. Life, whether it be fully lived or not, whether it be structured by a liberated heart and confidence in a better social and political future or structured by the conventions of Surrey, is fragile and vulnerable. The mistake of Surrey is its belief that it has achieved "solidity" and therefore can deny peril; deny, by logical extension, death. And were there no peril of death, a blind attitude toward the demands of the heart and a social insularity that rejects the world might not matter as much. Since Surrey's error, however, is so basic and deep, Lucy's heroism, which means battle with family and friends, who are allied with "the enemy within," is a fight in their behalf. And again, since Surrey in the novel is meant as a microcosm of much of the world, her heroic perception of the implications of peril is a battle for "the whole world."

George and Lucy marry, and the novel briefly glimpses them honeymooning in the Pension Bertolini—a minor technical addition by Forster, returning them in the last few pages to symbolic Italy. A larger implication of this happy ending, however, is that the intention of the novel —the expansion of humanism to mean that love and politics are synthetically one and that heroism therefore battles for both when upholding either one—has been achieved.

The process has of course depended on poetry, particularly upon the shaping and controlling power of Mr. Emerson's rhetoric. But absent in the novel is a kind of man whose impact on the twentieth-century world cannot be denied. He is unsympathetic to poetry as a means of revealing the truth about personal relations, social conditions, or political realities. Moreover, he regards *himself* as the actual hero of the modern world. Like Mr. Emerson, he is concerned with the present and future but can, with some show of plausibility, insist that they bear and will continue to carry *his* stamp. He is the man of affairs, the successful builder of financial empires. In the early years of the twentieth century, it was he who had, in fact, consummated the long process of turning England into a middle-class nation. Above the truly impoverished, the separations were primarily among different levels of a single class.

In *Howards End,* Forster gives such a man full scope to act and reveal himself. The demands of the "heart" arise again, partially in connection with this self-proclaimed hero of the modern world, but in a context different and more complex from that of *A Room with a View.* Deferring to the legitimate claims of the man of affairs, Forster gives social and economic realism, directly rendered—a free hand to explore the important human questions. In the end, however, through a subtle and hardly noticeable process, he concludes once more that these questions can be answered only through poetry.

There has been much dissatisfaction with *Howards End,* and a large part of this discontent is based on the belief that Forster attempted to write a novel concerned with social and economic realities transcending personal relations, and failed. If, however, the reader takes seriously the many connotations of "view," in *A Room with a View,* and believes that a vision of the future, one of the more important meanings of "view," is intrinsic to any realistic treatment of society, he confronts a question. How else, except through poetry, even in a novel saturated with social realism, can such a vision be conceived and transformed into imagery? The question, for Forster, is rhetorical, but a fully informed response to *Howards End* will require concurrence with his own answer.

"ONLY CONNECT . . ." This epigraph, on the title page, would seem to preclude all discussion about the theme of *Howards End*. But the novel has prompted an immense number of critical responses, and a great many of these are at loggerheads with each other.

Part of the reason why the true substance of *Howards End* remains elusive is that Forster probably put more into the novel than is concretely delineated, and that elements of the "more" do not line up neatly with each other. Another reason for the difficulty in saying what *Howards End* is "about" is that the phrase "only connect . . ." acquires differing connotations as the novel progresses, even though the phrase is quoted from the story itself. Some critics have assumed that if one thing ought to be connected with another, because of seeming affinity, Forster has indeed combined the two. Others have assumed that in the novel *opposites* connect and that when they do, synthesis results.

Another difficulty in this novel is the problem of class. *Howards End* is the first of Forster's novels in which class plays a central and consciously contrived role. At the beginning of Chapter VI, Forster says, "We are not concerned with the very poor. They are unthinkable, and only to be approached by the statistician or the poet. This story deals with gentlefolk, or with those who are obliged to pretend that they are gentlefolk." [1]

The story does in fact deal with three families, who are

placed in three divisions of the middle class. One family is the Schlegels, principally Margaret and Helen, who are cultivated, favored with sensibility, and supported by inherited money. Another family is the Wilcoxes: business men and imperialists, representatives of the "outer life," people who, with the important exception of Mrs. Wilcox, are distrustful of the "inner life" and indifferent to many of the things, principally the past and nature, Forster himself believes good. The third "family" is composed of Leonard Bast and Jacky. Leonard, a clerk, is living with Jacky, ten years his senior. In the course of the novel — when Leonard turns twenty-one — they marry. Of Leonard, Forster writes, "The boy . . . stood at the extreme verge of gentility." (*p. 48*).

The limits of the novel then, are the economic and social perimeters of the middle class at a time when the middle class constituted the economic, moral, and power center of England. The fact justifies in part Lionel Trilling's observation, "*Howards End* is a novel about England's fate. It is a story of the class war. . . . The symbol for England is the house whose name gives the title to the book . . . the plot of *Howards End* is about the rights of property. . . . [The novel] asks the question, 'Who shall inherit England?' " [2]

Many critics, accepting the question as a challenge, have gone on to criticize Forster's method of formulating the query and responding to it. As the story develops, the three families become interlocked, but at the conclusion, Howards End will be passed on to the illegitimate child of Helen Schlegel and Leonard Bast. Since the child is an undeveloped symbol of the future, a number of readers have found him an unsatisfactory answer.

At the outset we are therefore confronted with two problems. What, as the novel progresses, become the actual meanings of "Only connect . . ." as Forster's imagination, consciously and unconsciously, plays over the many possibilities of the concept? What, to name the second problem, is the actual status in the novel of Forster's realistic treatment of the middle class and the future of its England?

The first problem requires us to divest ourselves of the Hegelian and post-Hegelian idea that all pairs of antitheses necessarily lead to syntheses. In *Howards End,* one device that creates the concrete building blocks of the plot is the pitting against each other of hard, impermeable opposites. *Howards End* is filled with insoluble dilemmas—antitheses that structure the plot but lead to no realistic syntheses.

An important confrontation of such opposites is unwittingly anticipated early in the novel by the intellectual, cultivated, and idealistic Margaret Schlegel. She is discussing with Helen the Wilcoxes, who are business men and financial imperialists. "The truth is," Margaret says, "that there is a great outer life that you and I have never touched—a life in which telegrams and anger count. Personal relations, that we think supreme, are not supreme there. There love means marriage settlements . . . death duties. . . . This outer life, though obviously horrid, often seems the real one—there's grit in it. It does breed character" (*p. 28*).

Later in the novel, Margaret will attempt to "connect" this outer life with the personal relations that are, indeed, supreme to Helen and herself. Her idealistic aspirations, a kind of ambition, will cause her to believe that a synthesis of fundamentally opposite and contrasting characters, personalities, and values is possible. She will fail to impose her belief upon reality, and her failure will constitute an important part of the theme of *Howards End,* as well as a comment on reality itself.

The first episode of the novel throws the Schlegels and the Wilcoxes together. At a time prior to the story, the two families had met on the Continent. Back in England, the Wilcoxes invite the Schlegel sisters to Howards End, but only Helen is able to go. She impulsively becomes engaged—for a day—to the younger of the two sons, Paul.

Through this episode we not only witness Forster's skill and pleasure at domestic comedy but become acquainted with other characters in the novel: the sisters' aunt, Mrs. Munt; the older of the Wilcox brothers, Charles; and Mrs. Wilcox.

In addition, Forster uses Helen's flash romance to contrast the two sisters and to establish in the novel another dichotomy: "The sisters were alike as little girls, but at the time of the Wilcox episode their methods were beginning to diverge; the younger [Helen] was rather apt to entice people, and, in enticing them, to be herself enticed; the elder went straight ahead and accepted an occasional failure as part of the game" (*p.* 32). James Hall has commented, "The truly interested writing in *Howards End* . . . is about intellectual versus intellectual—the split between Margaret and Helen over how life should be lived." [3] There are other important "splits" in the novel, but Hall has identified one of them.

The class antithesis between Leonard Bast and the Schlegels is of course different from the conflict between the sisters and the Wilcoxes. Money—or lack of it— determines many aspects of the Schlegel-Bast relationship.

The sisters meet Leonard at a concert hall, in which the notable description of Helen's experience of Beethoven's Fifth Symphony also takes place. The Symphony concluded, Helen—in a revery—leaves. She absent-mindedly takes Leonard Bast's umbrella. Leonard mentions this to Margaret, and during her efforts to arrange for its return, Leonard struggles with the suspicion that the confidence trick has been played upon him. Forster uses the incident to delineate a difference between the Schlegels and Leonard, all members of the middle class. "To trust people is a luxury in which only the wealthy can indulge; the poor cannot afford it" (*p.* 37).

The ability to "trust" is a matter of character, of morality and manners. Forster expands the antithesis between Leonard and the Schlegels. "He knew that he was poor, and would admit it: he would have died sooner than confess any inferiority to the rich. . . . But he was inferior to most rich people. . . . He was not as courteous . . . nor as intelligent, nor as healthy, nor as lovable. . . . But in his day the angel of Democracy had arisen . . . proclaiming, 'All men are equal—all men, that is to say, who possess umbrellas,' and so he was obliged to assert gentility, lest he slipped into the abyss where nothing counts, and the statements of Democracy are inaudible" (*p. 48*).

Forster's unsentimental realism, acutely transforming class into manners, character, health, and security, is given its full economic dimension by Margaret, speaking to Mrs. Munt. "You and I and the Wilcoxes stand upon money as upon islands. It is so firm beneath our feet that we forget its very existence. It's only when we see someone near us tottering that we realize all that an independent income means. Last night . . . I began to think that the very soul of the world is economic, and that the lowest abyss is not the absence of love, but the absence of coin" (*p. 64*). Later, Margaret voices a provocative epigram, "Cash . . . is the warp of civilization, whatever the woof may be" (*p. 134*).

Margaret's aphorisms, even though some are proved wrong, help *Howards End* to proceed on two levels. The first is social and economic realism. The other is best alluded to, for the moment, by negation. Coin, on this second level, is not the soul of the world, and the "woof" is not subject to infinite variety. The gift of a special imagination, it is Forster's own providing.

On the realistic level, however, the right-angled opposition between the warp and the woof suggests an antithesis. The same meeting at right angles, connoting the impossibility of merging into one, is expressed when Mr. Wilcox and his children, who have been motoring and have had a collision with a country cart, recount the incident to Mrs. Wilcox, "—Cart and car being practically at right angles—" (*p. 92*). Lionel Trilling has observed that "in 1910 the automobile is already the totem of the Wilcox males," [4] and throughout the novel the automobile is in antagonistic contact with opposites that cannot merge or synthesize with this emblem of the business class.

Another important antithesis is between Howards End and London, eternal foes. Among other meanings, Howards End stands for country peace and grace, for continuity and direction, for the highest type of humanity Forster can envision in 1910. London is its direct opposite, "One visualizes it as a tract of quivering grey, intelligent without purpose, and excitable without love; as a spirit that has altered before it can be chronicled; as a heart that certainly beats, but with no pulsation of humanity" (*p.* 114).

There is even a conflict among the meanings of Leonard Bast's role. Defined by social and economic realism, Leonard is clear. But on another level, he acquires different meanings, one reason why unsympathetic critics of *Howards End* regard it as unsatisfactory.

An early indication of the transfiguration Leonard is to experience is rooted in realism itself. The evidence is indirectly disclosed by the umbrella incident. Margaret, after the concert, has given him her card and has invited him to Wickham Place, the Schlegels' home, to retrieve his umbrella. The Schlegels find Leonard "interesting," and he remains on their minds.

In a chance meeting with Mr. Wilcox the sisters are told that the Porphyrion, the insurance company for which Leonard works, is about to fold. Aroused, they invite Leonard to Wickham Place a second time, determined to warn him. For Leonard, however, the sisters represent culture, with the special connotation of aspiration that culture has for him. In a comic, less than half-tragic, scene, in which he wants to talk culture with these exalted beings and they want to urge him to leave his Company, Leonard is upset and annoyed by the way the Schlegels persistently return to the subject of his job. "He did not want Romance to collide with the Porphyrion . . . they to him were denizens of Romance, who must keep to the corner he had assigned them, pictures that must not walk out of their frames" (*pp.* 129–30). In other contexts in the novel, romance will have other meanings. Here it is a subtle spirit, emanating from Leonard's low social and economic base, and not only widening the gulf between him and the sisters but raising questions about the relation between social class and perceptions of reality.

Sex, too, creates an antithesis in the novel. Male and female never realistically "merge," despite frequent references to the body and to breeding. During the episode in which Leonard has been invited to Wickham Place to be warned about the Porphyrion, Mr. Wilcox, accompanied by his daughter, Evie, makes an appearance. After a tangle of misunderstandings, tragic and comic at once, Leonard leaves in a huff. Mr. Wilcox has assumed that the sisters have merely been "handling" an outrageously impertinent member of a lower class. Margaret corrects him and tells him, finally, that Leonard is a real man. "As she spoke their eyes met, and it was as if Mr. Wilcox's defences fell. She saw back to the real man in him. . . . A woman and two men — they had formed the magic triangle of sex, and the male was thrilled to jealousy, in case the female was attracted by another male" (*p.* 156).

In addition to adding a new diagram, the "triangle," jealousy foreshadows the role that the idea of possession will play in the "connection" of the sexes. Possession implies, at best, desire to control someone different from oneself. It implies, at worst, desire that the possessed lose all identity, become an incorporated extension of the possessor. It does not imply synthesis.

The Arnoldian goal — to see life steadily and see it whole — contributes to the antitheses in *Howards End.* Leonard, we are told, aspires to the goal, and, realistically, fails. Of Margaret and Mr. Wilcox, Forster says, "It is impossible to see modern life steadily and see it whole, and she had chosen to see it whole. Mr. Wilcox saw steadily. He never bothered over the mysterious or the private" (*pp.* 170–71).

In the course of the novel, the first Mrs. Wilcox dies, and the passage of time and the structure of the plot join in causing Mr. Wilcox to propose marriage to Margaret, who accepts. She does not love him but believes that she can totally understand him and can create within him the connection that serves as the epigraph for the novel. "Mature as he was, she might yet be able to help him to the building of the rainbow bridge that should connect the prose in us with the passion. Without it we are meaningless fragments, half monks, half beasts, unconnected arches that have never joined into a man" (*p. 196*). And, "It did not seem so difficult. . . . She would only point out the salvation that was latent in his own soul. . . . Only connect! That was the whole of her sermon. . . . Only connect, and the beast and the monk robbed of the isolation that is life to either, will die" (*p. 197*).

Here then, is the central reference to "connecting" in *Howards End*. Whatever Forster's conscious intentions, however, the quoted passage is the ultimate of the antithesis leading to no syntheses. Realistically, "prose" and "poetry" remain inviolable opposites, connecting only in the sense that their surfaces, when brought into direct contact, merely clash.

One more set of antitheses in the novel will be cited. "The Imperialist and the Yeoman: these are the real antagonists of the novel." [5] Every critical reader finds his own set of primary opposites in *Howards End*; but this one is particularly telling. Leonard Bast is descended from the yeomanry. Ruth Wilcox—the first Mrs. Wilcox—is the last of a particular line of the yeomanry, the Howards. The Schlegel sisters are descended, on their mother's side, from the yeomanry. In contrast, Henry Wilcox and his children quintessentially express the Imperialist class. Throughout the novel, there is only diagrammatic opposition and clash—never merger or synthesis—between the Imperialist and the Yeoman.

Yet "connections" do occur in *Howards End*. However, when they do, it is for the sake of irony. Such connections reinforce the insufficiency of the middle class and of Margaret's theory concerning the power of intellect and sensibility to transcend society's ills.

An early instance of ironic connection occurs when Mrs. Munt, who has arrived at Howards End to investigate the startling news that Helen is engaged to Paul, is met by Charles Wilcox, whom she mistakes for Paul and who is ignorant of the engagement. As Mrs. Munt and Charles talk, in a scene of expert domestic comedy, the true nature of the situation becomes disentangled from ignorance and presumption. Anger on both sides commences. "So they played the game of Capping Families. . . . They played it

with unusual vigour, stating in so many words that Schlegels were better than Wilcoxes, Wilcoxes better than
Schlegels. They flung decency aside. The man was young,
the woman deeply stirred; in both a vein of coarseness was
latent" (*p. 22*). The vein of coarseness in Mrs. Munt will
never figure so prominently again, but the connection
hints at the many parallel inadequacies in Wilcoxes and
Schlegels that will be revealed as the novel progresses.

An aphorism, links through art, the Wilcoxes and Schlegels. "Henry only censured the lower classes when it suited
him. . . . 'I have patience with a man who knows his job,'
he would say, really having patience with the job, and not
the man. Paradoxical as it may sound, he had something
of the artist about him; he would pass over an insult to his
daughter sooner than lose a good charwoman for his wife"
(*pp. 280–81*). The sisters, especially Margaret, are, of
course, devoted to art.

There are many kinds of symbols in the novel,[6] but
Cyrus Hoy has singled out some of the associations between symbolism and ironic connection. Notably, these
associations occur through Forster's use of glass. When
Margaret travels to Shropshire, to attend Evie Wilcox's
wedding, Forster describes the railroad car Mr. Wilcox has
ordered for the guests. "The long glass saloon, that moved
so easily and felt so comfortable, became a forcing-house
for the idea of sex" (*p. 222*). Hoy observes, "It is in just
such an enclosure as this that the first Mrs. Wilcox has
passed the days of her married life. Margaret, watching
the glass doors of the elevator close upon the figure of
Mrs. Wilcox . . . had felt for her 'the sense of an impris-
onment.'" And further, "on separate but parallel occasions in the novel, glass is broken and blood is shed by
. . . Margaret Schlegel and Leonard Bast. . . . Back in his
flat after his first visit to the Schlegels, Leonard knocks to
the floor a photograph of . . . Jacky, cuts his fingers. . . .
Margaret, visiting Mrs. Wilcox is shown a double frame
containing photographs of Charles Wilcox and his recent
bride Dolly. This she drops, smashes Dolly's glass, and
cuts her finger on the fragments." [7]

What are we to conclude from these parallels? Primarily that Basts, Wilcoxes, and Schlegels are ironically linked, through the symbol of glass, as people equally inadequate sexually—despite Margaret's superior ability to envision the connecting rainbow.

Another ironic connection creates a parallel between Helen and the Wilcoxes, presumably the two most antithetical forces in *Howards End*. Just before the first Mrs. Wilcox dies, she writes on a scrap of paper—her will—a request to her family that Margaret Schlegel be given Howards End. The Wilcoxes burn the paper, and to quiet the faint stirring of conscience, send Margaret Mrs. Wilcox's silver vinaigrette. Helen, after she has impulsively given herself sexually to a ruined Leonard Bast (he left the Porphyrion, after all, but lost his new job, while the Porphyrion prospered) and has then fled, tries to send him money. Ironic connection is again evident: "[Helen] tries to salve her conscience with a gift of money, a parallel situation to Henry's sending Margaret the vinaigrette." [8]

At the concert hall in which the Schlegels first meet Leonard, Helen notices disapprovingly that the ceiling displays painted cupids. Later, Forster introduces us into the interior of Leonard's apartment and writes that "one [wall] was occupied . . . by a draped mantelshelf bristling with Cupids" (*p.* 50). Frederic McDowell notes, "[Helen's] distaste for the painted cupids on the ceiling of the concert hall—she would hate to marry a man like them—connects with the fact that Leonard, the only man with whom she becomes sexually intimate, himself has 'a draped mantelshelf bristling with Cupids.' . . . Meanwhile she has failed to see how her carelessness in running off with the return tickets from Shropshire and forgetting to pay the hotel bill is immediately more ruinous for Leonard than his dismissal from the bank." [9] The ironic connection can be continued: Helen's carelessness parallels Mr. Wilcox's thoughtless indifference to Leonard's immediate plight. It was Mr. Wilcox who gave the erroneous advice about the Porphyrion.

An irony sharply defining the limited power of Marga-

ret's intellectual, imaginative sensibility reveals itself earlier, before her marriage, when she is inspecting Mr.
Wilcox's house in Ducie Street, to which she has come
with the intention of subletting. Wickham Place, the
original Schlegel home, is to be torn down.

Henry exploits Margaret's house-hunting as a ruse to
draw her into his Ducie Street house, where he offers
marriage. Before he does propose and as Margaret inspects
the diningroom, Forster writes, "The room suggested
men, and Margaret, keen to derive the modern capitalist
from the warriors and hunters of the past, saw it as an
ancient guest-hall, where the lord sat at meat among his
thanes" (*p.* 172). A moment later, Henry proposes. The
irony is that Margaret, the center of sensibility in the
novel, has linked Henry with the English nobles of
the past. If anything is certain, it is that Forster regards
the character of historic and mythic nobles as diametri-
cally opposed to the character of the early twentieth-
century Imperialists—of Henry Wilcox.

An entire series of ironic connections near the end of
the novel condenses and intensifies feeling and meaning.
Through a scheme of Henry's, Helen, mysteriously absent
for months, has been brought to Howards End. He believes that she is mentally unbalanced and must be captured through guile and delivered into the hands of a
doctor.

Earlier in the novel, we learn that Jacky Bast was once
the mistress of Henry Wilcox. After much difficulty, Margaret had succeeded in making Henry feel that she had
forgiven him, and their marriage had taken place on
schedule. At Howards End, Margaret discovers the reason
for her sister's strange silence and absence; Helen is pregnant with Leonard's child. Margaret immediately transfers
her loyalty from Henry to Helen. The sisters decide to
spend one night together at Howards End, but Margaret
still feels that Henry's permission must be obtained. For
reasons that have their roots in many events and aspects of
character established early in the novel, Henry refuses.
Margaret explodes.

You shall see the connection if it kills you . . . ! You have had a mistress—I forgave you. My sister has a lover—you drive her from the house. Do you see the connection? . . .—a man who insults his wife when she's alive and cants with her memory when she is dead. A man who ruins a woman for his pleasure, and casts her off to ruin other men. And gives bad financial advice, and then says he is not responsible. These men are you. You can't recognize them, because you cannot connect (*p. 325*).

K. W. Gransden succinctly notes the ironic connections, "When Margaret asks if she and her sister may spend a night at Howards End, Henry refuses his second wife's request as he had refused the last request of his first wife." And, "Charged with failure to connect, Henry goes on not connecting. There must still be one law for him and another for Helen, even though the connexion could hardly be made more obvious for him: for his mistress is now the wife of Helen's lover." [10]

Another richly complex irony is unwittingly conveyed by Henry himself. It is the middle of the night. Margaret is absent. Henry says to Charles, " 'I am morally certain that she is with her sister at Howards End. The house is mine—and, Charles, it will be yours—and when I say that no one is to live there, I mean that no one is to live there. I won't have it.' He looked angrily at the moon. 'To my mind this question is connected with something far greater, the rights of property itself' " (*p. 344*).

Forster's accomplishment is threefold. At the height of the drama of personal relations, he has reminded us that *Howards End* concerns attitudes toward property. He has comically created an incongruity—Henry staring angrily, but insensibly, at the perennial Romantic symbol, the moon. Finally, Forster has used this symbol of the mysterious as a reminder that *Howards End*, concerned with the insufficiencies of the middle class, will also suggest that the power of literary realism to expose them is limited.

There is ironic connection in the violence that occurs shortly before the novel concludes. Leonard, in an agony of conscience over what he regards as his sin against

Helen, goes down to Howards End to confess. He arrives just as Charles, who has been sent by his father to remove Helen, is berating the sisters.

When Leonard appears, Charles, convinced that Leonard is part of a vulgar scheme on the part of the Schlegels, snatches up the sword of Ernst Schlegel, the soldier-idealist father of the sisters, and strikes Leonard with its flat. The sword had been hung above the Schlegel books. The arrangement had been made by Miss Avery, who is an elderly charwoman, but more important, a descendant of the yeoman class, like Ruth Wilcox. Leonard falls, pulls the books down with him, and dies, actually of a heart attack. "It is a sword wielded by one of the Wilcoxes, the new conquerors of England, which has in effect killed Leonard, and it is the books of the Schlegels, representative of the culture he has aspired to, which symbolically bury him." [11]

A final word about "connecting" in *Howards End*. Besides irreconcilable antitheses and ironic connections, there is, in fact, realistic union, although it is morally different from what Margaret had intended. After Leonard's death, Charles is imprisoned for three years, Henry breaks down, and Margaret establishes a new household at Howards End. It consists of an invalided Henry, Helen, Helen's baby boy, and Margaret herself. Earlier, during the first night that Margaret and Helen had spent together at Howards End, the sisters had discussed the past. They had referred to the episode in Shropshire, at the time of Evie's wedding, when Helen had brought along the ruined Basts and had demanded justice. Margaret had succeeded in getting Henry to agree to give Leonard a clerk's position in his own company. Then Jacky, drunk, had recognized her old lover, "Hen," and in the ensuing catastrophes Margaret had concentrated all her efforts on helping Henry rebuild his defenses. She had sent Leonard a note, enclosed in a letter to Helen, curtly advising him that Mr. Wilcox could not help at present, thereby sacrificing not only the Basts but Helen, for the sake of Henry.

The letters, as much as anything else, caused Helen to try to expiate what she believed to be the combined guilt of the Schlegels and Wilcoxes, by giving herself to Leonard. At Howards End, together again with Margaret, Helen says, "One isolates. . . . I isolated Mr. Wilcox from the other forces that were pulling Leonard downhill." Margaret then speaks of the letters, informing Helen that the idea of sending them was her own. Margaret says, "Looking back, that was wrong of me." Helen answers, "Looking back, darling, I know that it was right. It is right to save the man whom one loves. I am less enthusiastic about justice now" (*p. 330*).

Helen has pronounced the central moral truth of *Howards End* considered as a work of realism. She has said, in effect, that "connecting"—i.e., love—necessarily involves exclusion. Every act of connection simultaneously involves injustice to someone. Love and justice are also antitheses.

The point is reiterated at the end of the novel. Mr. Wilcox has called his family together and has told his children the conditions of his will: all his money to the Wilcoxes; Howards End to be left to Margaret, "[She] did not answer. There was something uncanny in her triumph. She, who had never expected to conquer anyone, had charged straight through these Wilcoxes and broken up their lives" (*pp. 360–61*).

What price, then, "connecting"? Unsympathetic characters as they are, the Wilcox children have certainly been excluded. They are deprived of the house that was originally their mother's property (actually, Ruth Wilcox's affection for Margaret was a first attempt to deny them their "realistic" inheritance). We are given to understand that father and children will henceforth see little, if anything, of each other.

And to cap this hard fact—that connecting also means excluding—Forster accentuates how very limited indeed is the connection that has finally been established between the invalided Henry and Margaret. The empty-minded Dolly, Charles' wife, blurts out: "It does seem curious . . . that Mrs. Wilcox should have left Margaret Howards End, and yet she got it, after all" (*p. 361*).

When all have left, Margaret says, "Could you tell me, Henry, what was that about Mrs. Wilcox having left me Howards End?" And, "Tranquilly he replied: 'Yes, she did. But that is a very old story. When she was ill and you were so kind to her she wanted to make you some return, and, not being herself at the time, scribbled 'Howards End' on a piece of paper. I went into it thoroughly, and, as it was clearly fanciful, I set it aside, little knowing what my Margaret would be to me in the future.' " Forster continues, "Margaret was silent. Something shook her life in its inmost recesses, and she shivered." Henry says, "I didn't do wrong, did I?" Margaret's reply sums up more than this particular conversation, "You didn't, darling. Nothing has been done wrong" (*p. 362*).

From one viewpoint, Margaret is right, but a realistic moral, social, and psychological assessment of the theme "Only connect . . ." concludes that she has given up hope of ever connecting with Henry, to say nothing of relating within him the beast and the monk, both enfeebled beyond repair. There is an odd affinity between Forster's first two published novels and *Howards End*. In each, the poetically inspired intellect and imagination lose hope in their visions.

The novel's final words depict a tableau, already noted as one of Forster's favorite devices. At the least, a tableau is allegorical, and Forster intends his to be symbolic, as well. "From the garden came laughter. . . . Helen rushed into the gloom, holding Tom by one hand and carrying her baby on the other. There were shouts of infectious joy." Then, " 'The field's cut!' Helen cried excitedly—'the big meadow! We've seen to the very end, and it'll be such a crop of hay as never!' " (*p. 362*).

The most common and obvious interpretation of the scene—Helen holding Tom by one hand and her baby on the other—is that Forster is offering an image of hope. The agricultural past has been linked to the classless baby, who is the future of England. Thus, England will rejuvenate herself by rooting her future in her best tradition.

As a realistic symbol of hope the scene doesn't work, nor has history supported its prophecy. But the presence of Tom in the tableau opens a view. Nephew of Miss Avery, Tom is an authentic representative of the yeoman class, and his presence, besides being a realistic fact, permits another way of looking at the conclusion—and thus at the entire novel.

Since there is nothing more "realistic" than class, those who are dissatisfied with *Howards End* have knowingly or unknowingly complained that Forster did not, at the conclusion, realistically prophesy a process of changes, in class structure, leading to England's rejuvenation. However, the complaint places upon the novelistic imagination an impossible demand. Further, it does not necessarily follow that Forster, because he was aware of the insufficiencies of the middle class, felt obliged, in *Howards End*, even to attempt a remedy. His obligation was to write a novel that would emerge from whatever his intelligence perceived and from whatever visions his imagination conceived for moral purposes, whether those visions were as realistic as the facts disclosed by his intelligence or not.

Howards End does contain images and values that have no socially or politically realistic relevance to the twentieth century but are nevertheless posited—imaginatively and metaphorically—as the cure for the insufficiency of the middle class. The term that most inclusively describes this cluster of images and values is "aristocratic." Moreover, technically, they constitute the actual syntheses in *Howards End*: the images of aristocracy are created by an expert merging of realism and myth—or the poetic or ideal.

The first reference to "aristocracy" occurs early in the novel, when Mrs. Munt has come down to Howards End to rescue Helen and has arrived at the house embroiled in an argument with Charles, into which the anxious Paul has been drawn. Ruth Wilcox approaches, "trailing noiselessly over the lawn, and there was actually a wisp of hay in her hands. She seemed to belong not to the young people and their motor, but to the house, and to the tree that overshadowed it. One knew that she worshipped the past, and that the instinctive wisdom the past can alone bestow had descended upon her—that wisdom to which we give the clumsy name of aristocracy. High born she might not be. But assuredly she cared about her ancestors, and let them help her. When she saw Charles angry, Paul frightened, and Mrs. Munt in tears, she heard her ancestors say, 'Separate those human beings who will hurt each other most. The rest can wait' " (*p. 23*).

The real and the ideal have been effectively synthesized, even as two "realities" seldom are in the novel. Realistically, Mrs. Wilcox is the last of a line of yeomanry, not of the literal aristocracy. But her instincts and manners are those which have, mythically, always been attributed to an aristocracy, whether it be social and political, intellectual, or moral. There is even an historical interpretation that is quite apposite here. Forster's interest in Samuel Butler has been noted. Some critics have seen an even more direct influence of Butler upon Forster than he has acknowledged. Of the period in which Forster was writing *Howards End*, Angus Wilson has said, "Butler's ideas, which were essentially aristocratic, had . . . become attached to the doctrines of Socialism and so married to other channels of liberalism, tolerance, and philanthropy." [12]

Whether or not Forster would acknowledge that his own temperament and vision were formed by this process, an analagous fact suggests itself. He has implied in some of his statements that the roots of his humanistic creed are in the Renaissance, surely a period when humanism and aristocracy were closer together than they have ever again been in Western history.

Closely allied to Mrs. Wilcox, in the structure and moral meaning of the novel, is Ernst Schlegel, the father of Margaret and Helen, and dead before the events of *Howards End*. He had been a soldier in pre-1870 Germany; he had also been an idealist. "If one classed him at all it would be as the countryman of Hegel and Kant, as the idealist . . . whose Imperialism was . . . of the air. Not that his life had been inactive. He had fought like blazes against Denmark, Austria, France. But he had fought without visualizing the results of victory. A hint of

the truth broke on him after Sedan. . . . Peace came—
. . . one had turned into an Empire—but he knew that
some quality [imagination] had vanished. . . . he . . .
naturalized himself in England . . ." (*pp. 29–30*).

Ernst Schlegel's activism, idealism, and imagination
connect with the ancestral wisdom of Ruth Wilcox. They
also oppose Mr. Schlegel to the Wilcox males, who are
precisely the kind of unimaginative empire-builders he has
sought to escape by emigrating to England.

A "soldier-idealist," however, is a synthesis of the real
and the mythic, and the fact indicates again that Forster's
images of nobility are aesthetically contrived—mergers of
social realism and myth. What is most important is that
within the limits of fiction, the contrivance is convincing.

Everything that has been said so far about Forster's
conception of the "aristocratic" prevents us from placing
it in any fixed moment of history, though some of its
realistic antecedents—the tradition of the English countryside, the idealism in continental Romantic culture—have
been suggested.

But one aspect of Ernst Schlegel's aristocracy—he is,
realistically, as middle class as the Wilcoxes—is his attitude toward his fellow humans. At one point, Margaret
says, "You remember how [father] would trust strangers,
and if they fooled him he would say, 'It's better to be
fooled than to be suspicious'—that the confidence trick is
the work of man, but the want-of-confidence trick is the
work of the devil" (*p. 44*). It would be difficult to place
such an attitude historically, but the aspiration toward
maintaining one's "best self" and the rhetorical reference
to religion suggest Matthew Arnold and the implicit aristocracy of mind and morality in his critique of the nineteenth-century English middle class.[13]

A direct, if rhetorical, link between the aristocratic and
Ernst Schlegel is suggested by Forster himself, drawing his
imagery from the Middle Ages, as he did for a similar
purpose in *A Room with a View*. When the Schlegel
sisters are about to be evicted from Wickham Place,
which will be torn down in the name of progress and

replaced by a row of flats, Forster writes, "The feudal ownership of land did bring dignity, whereas the modern ownership of movables is reducing us again to a nomadic horde. We are reverting to the civilization of luggage, and historians of the future will note how the middle classes accreted possessions without taking root in the earth, and may find in this the secret of their imaginative poverty. The Schlegels were certainly the poorer for the loss of Wickham Place. It had helped to balance their lives, and almost to counsel them." (*p.* 158). Ruth Wilcox is the only character actually present in the novel who can be said to have "dignity," but Mr. Schlegel established Margaret and Helen in Wickham Place and his remembered words "counsel" them as much as the house does.

Margaret, under the pressures of early twentieth-century social reality, chooses to see life whole, and Henry, less consciously, sees it steadily. But Arnold's concept had become an aristocratic myth by 1910. Thus, for fictional purposes, Forster creates another characteristic synthesis of the real and the ideal when Margaret thinks of the remaining farms of the English yeomanry. "In these English farms, if anywhere, one might see life steadily and see it whole, group in one vision its transitoriness and its eternal youth, connect—connect without bitterness until all men are brothers" (*pp.* 283–84). As a prescription for the future of England, Margaret's thought and feeling are meaningless; as poetic statement grounded in realistic imagery they are as realistic as moral sensibility itself.

Miss Avery is a minor but additional example of synthesis. "She looked capable of scathing wit and also of high but unostentatious nobility" (*p.* 287). Like Ruth Wilcox, she is descended from the yeomanry. She too is gifted with wisdom at once preternatural and grounded in realistic history. It is she who sets up the symbolic arrangement, Ernst Schlegel's sword of adventurous and active idealism hanging over the books containing Western culture. And she in effect tells Margaret that the future of England ought to have been ensured by the union of a man like Ernst Schlegel and a woman like Ruth Wilcox (*p. 290*). Her conviction prompts in Margaret the realization that a modern Imperialist is not the historical descendant of an aristocrat but the inexorable antithesis of the whole cluster of mythic images and moral ideals that constitute the pale spirit of aristocracy in the England of 1910—a spirit that can exist only in literature.

Helen is a highly complex characterization. She commits many errors. But on that level of the novel where the real and the mythic combine, she is another aspect of aristocracy. She exhibits the heroism, the spirit of adventure, the striving for the ideal that create tragedy. And artistically, the possibility of tragedy is another element constituting the aristocratic in the novel.

John Beer writes, "The contrast between Helen and Margaret reflects a contrast that intrigues Forster: the contrast between the hero and the man of civilization. The hero strives after some absolute ideal and is therefore liable to perish in youth, physically or spiritually: the man of civilization is intent on establishing a way of life." [14] And "civilization," in *Howards End*, means the inadequate middle class, amenable to no realistic vision of change.

Thus it is Helen who hears, from an essentially aristocratic point of view, the entire tragedy of human life, when she listens to Beethoven's Fifth Symphony; who hears the presence of the goblins—panic and emptiness; hears Beethoven's heroic honesty—admission that the goblins might return.

And in her fateful conversation with Leonard at the hotel she goes Margaret one better on the subject of money. Margaret's image of the warp and the woof is essentially an imaginative rendering of social realism, a statement that within the limits of middle-class society a civilized life can be lived if one has both money and a personal interest.

Helen's discussion of money transcends, morally and spiritually, the view of the best life possible within the inadequate middle class. Helen says to Leonard,

"Injustice and greed would be the real thing if we lived for ever. As it is, we must hold to other things, because Death is coming. I love Death—not morbidly, but because He explains. He shows me the emptiness of Money. Death and Money are the eternal foes. Not Death and Life, . . . Death destroys a man: the idea of Death saves him . . . Death is [Love's] foe, but his peer, and in their age-long struggle the thews of Love have been strengthened, and his vision cleared, until there is no one who can stand against him." (*pp.* 252–53).

In *Howards End*, money and death are real. But Helen's love of the *idea* of death has the tone of aristocratic myth. So, too, does her vision of death vanquished by love. She is attempting a viable heroism. But a heroine, essentially an aristocrat, can exist in *Howards End* precisely because she introduces into the story mythic feelings and ideas.

The characterization of Helen is also responsible for the addition of a heroic dimension to the realistically submerged Leonard Bast. Within the structure of the plot, Helen has conferred upon him the possibility of heroic tragedy.

On his first visit to the Schlegels, Leonard told them of his night-long tramp through the Surrey woods. Asked if the dawn was wonderful, he had answered, "No." He has been prepared at this point for a role that will transcend his socially realistic one. "He tests art by nature, and thus at once is one of Forster's saved; and the honesty of his response to what he sees impresses the sisters, and constitutes his 'epiphany' as a human being. It is his last and only moment of glory, but because of it he is worth saving." [15] If he if worth saving, from some point of view or upon some level of the novel, his first moment of glory will not be his last. Just before he sets out for Howards End to confess—and to meet his death—Forster describes him writhing in the agony of a sleepless night in his dreary flat. "In the horror. . . . [he] never confused the past. He remained alive, and blessed are those who live, if it is only to a sense of sinfulness. The anodyne of muddledom, by which most men blur and blend their mistakes, never passed Leonard's lips." And Forster quotes Meredith.

> *And if I drink oblivion of a day.*
> *So shorten I the stature of my soul.*

"It is a hard saying," writes Forster, "and a hard man wrote it, but it lies at the foot of all character" (*p. 336*). Leonard's achievement has no literal connection with the social realism characterizing him as an unhealthy, unintelligent, deprived clerk. But it prepares him for his tragic and therefore noble death at Howards End.

When he has arrived in Hertfordshire and is approaching the house, realism and poetry blend not only to develop his tragedy and heroism but to reinforce the antithesis between the Imperialist and the yeoman-aristocrat-idealist. "At the chalk-pit a motor passed [Leonard]. In it was another type, whom Nature favours—the Imperial. Healthy, ever in motion, it hopes to inherit the earth. . . . But the Imperialist is not what he thinks or seems. He is a destroyer. . . . To Leonard, intent on his private sin, there came the conviction of innate goodness elsewhere. . . . Again and again must the drums tap, and the goblins stalk over the universe before joy can be purged of the superficial. It was rather paradoxical, and arose from his sorrow. Death destroys a man, but the idea of death saves him—that is the best account of it that has yet been given. Squalor and tragedy can beckon to all that is great in us and strengthen the wings of love" (*p. 342*). Echoing Helen, he becomes a synthesis of realism and myth.

The image of Leonard in death completes his tragic and noble transfiguration. The image even suggests the effigy of a knight on a tomb in a cathedral. "There was nothing else to be done; the time for telegrams and anger was over, and it seemed wisest that the hands of Leonard should be folded on his breast and be filled with flowers. . . . Let Squalor be turned into Tragedy, whose eyes are the stars, and whose hands hold the sunset and the dawn" (*p. 349*).

We can now reconsider the realistically "unsatisfactory" tableau with which the novel concludes. Helen's classless child suggests also the possibility of a new elite, and one kind of elite or another always does emerge, once any given class structure is shattered.

The child is a mythic, "featureless" symbol of the future, and has nothing, as such, to do with the current of realism in *Howards End*. The realistic figure is Tom, the agricultural child whom Helen holds by one hand as she holds her symbolic, "unrealistic" baby in the other. In the final tableau Forster does what he has done throughout the novel. He creates an idea of aristocracy—here the idea of a future elite—by successfully synthesizing an element of social realism, Tom, with a mythic, symbolic element, Helen's baby.

Viewed in this manner, the conclusion asks us only to accept the fact that *Howards End* proceeds throughout on two levels: social realism and mythic incarnation of the idea of aristocracy—the only idea through which Forster can perceive and define the inadequacies of the middle class in 1910 and the severely limited hopes for its future offered by the energy of the Wilcoxes, the cultural sensibility of the Schlegels, and the decency and aspiration of the Leonard Basts.[16]

History since 1910 has often been used in the service of a negative critique of the novel. But history, like all other creations of man, is his servant. Beginning with critical principles discarded by those who see *Howards End* only as a failure in the genre of social and moral realism, we can call on history to confirm the persistent emergence of new elites and to approve Forster's synthetic method of adumbrating the one to come—the one that is still "featureless."

IT IS NATURAL to seek, in A *Passage to India*, a final fictional statement of Forster's themes and concerns. Published in 1924, fourteen years after *Howards End*, A *Passage to India* has remained the last of Forster's completed and published novels. Because one seeks a dramatic climax in the fictional career of a man whose novels have become classics in his own lifetime, it is natural also to see in A *Passage to India* an achievement that passes the mark set by Forster's other novels.

Neither expectation need disappoint. Read against the background of the earlier novels, A *Passage to India* reveals all that the critical impulse to synthesize and set in meaningful order desires. However, A *Passage to India* can also be discussed as an isolated achievement. Any approach permitting the exploration of the novel in a liberal manner is justifiable.

The plot is divided into three parts: "Mosque"; "Caves"; "Temple"; and the story is set in India. In his notes to the Everyman Edition (1957), Forster has said, "The three sections . . . also represent the three seasons of the Cold Weather, the Hot Weather, and the Rains, which divide the Indian year." [1]

Within this structure, the lives and relationships of certain Englishmen and Indians are played out. The central figures are Cyril Fielding, a decent, intellectual Englishman who is in the Indian city of Chandrapore as principal of the Government (English) school; and Aziz,

a Moslem doctor with whom Fielding attempts friendship. Another English resident-ruler is Ronnie Heaslop,
City Magistrate. Ronnie's twice-widowed mother, Mrs.
Moore, has accompanied to India Adela Quested, who
has come out so that she and Ronnie can decide whether
or not they wish to marry. Most of the English in
Chandrapore look down upon the Indians—Hindus and
Moslems, but Fielding, Adela, and Mrs. Moore desire
their friendship.

Out of this desire arises the famous expedition to the
Marabar Caves. Aziz has arranged the outing, and when
Fielding, held up by an Indian Brahman-professor, Dr.
Godbole, misses the train, Aziz conducts Adela and Mrs.
Moore to the caves. In the first cave visited, Mrs. Moore
hears a disquieting echo and declines to explore any fur-
ther. Aziz and Adela, accompanied by a single Indian
guide, go on alone. In a mix-up, they enter different caves.
Adela, highly strung, in part because of her confused
emotions toward Ronnie, thinks she has been attacked.

Back in Chandrapore, she accuses Aziz. Among the
English, only Fielding (who had joined the outing later)
believes Aziz innocent. A trial is held, and at its height,
Adela, under intense strain, recovers from her delusion
and repudiates her accusation. She and Fielding leave
India (Mrs. Moore had been packed off before the trial
started and had died at sea). Dr. Godbole and Aziz trans-
fer to the Indian state of Mau, Godbole to teach and Aziz
to become the Hindu ruler's physician.

We are now in the third section, "Temple." The yearly
religious rites, celebrating the birth of the god Krishna, are
in progress. Fielding, who has married Mrs. Moore's
daughter, Stella, has returned to India, and accompanied
by his wife and her brother, Ralph, is visiting Mau.

A great deal of misunderstanding after the trial had
separated Fielding and Aziz. Principally, Aziz had allowed
himself to believe, refusing to read the letters he had
received from England, that Fielding had married Adela.
At the conclusion of the Indian rites, characterized by
public confusion, the private error concerning Fielding's

marriage is cleared up; Aziz and Fielding attempt friendship once more. The attempt fails.

When first published in 1924, A *Passage to India* was a popular success, based in large part on the assumption that the novel was political. But Forster has corrected this misconception: "In writing it . . . my main purpose was not political, was not even sociological."[2] And Lionel Trilling has written, "Great as the problem of India is, Forster's book is not about India alone: it is about all of human life."[3] Particularly at this date, there can be no quarrel with Trilling's assessment. But what, according to Forster, is all human life *about*? Wary as we have become, we still ask this question when we read any great novel that is in the humanist tradition. Paradoxically, Forster, one of the most deeply committed humanists of the twentieth century, as well as one of the most sophisticated, seems to evade the question throughout *Passage*. Nevertheless, his intellect and his moral vision do provide an answer, almost despite his deliberate conception of the novel.

Forster's biography is an obvious aid to discussing *Passage*. But Forster has been so copious and generous in telling us about his Indian experiences,[4] many of which, properly altered for aesthetic purposes, appear in the novel, that it is useless to select schematically from his recorded observations and memories. Nonetheless, in Forster's autobiographical relation to India are facts literally relevant to the novel. In his recollections, moreover, Forster has referred directly to *Passage*.

In his years of active novel writing, Forster paid two visits to the Indian state of Dewas Senior. The first was in 1912–1913, the second in 1921, when he served as the ruler's private secretary. "I began [*Passage*] before my 1921 visit, and took out the opening chapters with me. . . . But . . . confronted with the country they purported to describe, they seemed to . . . go dead and I could do nothing with them. . . . The gap between India remembered and . . . experienced was too wide. When I got back to England the gap narrowed, and I was able to resume."[5]

If the "gap narrowed" only when he was back in England, a number of possibilities suggest themselves. To order the emotional substance of *Passage*, he may have needed a tranquility not provided by India. The immediacy of sad India's masses of humanity may have overwhelmed his cherished belief in the individual. He may, too, have been weaving into the fabric of the novel a particular theory requiring—for transformation into plot, character, scene, and mood—distance from its inspiration.

The last possibility encourages a specific approach to *Passage*. Like the appraisal of *The Longest Journey*, an exploration of *Passage* should be directed primarily to the novel's interrelated themes. Although Forster seems at times to discourage this approach—to confront it with diversions or misdirections—it leads to his own moral and metaphysical certainties. These hold the novel together.

An imposing fact about *Passage* is that out of the previous contest between illusion and reality, conceivably the theme of Forster's first four novels, a new, enlarged reality has emerged. It embraces much previously assigned to illusion. But this expansion of reality creates a dramatic threat. When reality, an omnivorous concept in India, begins to absorb illusion itself, reality is imperiled in a manner hitherto unknown in Forster's novels. It is eventually saved, but not by defeating or "exposing" illusion. It is saved when it learns or remembers its own attributes and limits; when it learns not to devour illusion but to accommodate itself to living, with as much confidence as it can muster, side by side with it.

The achievement requires intellectual strategy, the use of post-metaphysical empiricism. A grasp of this philosophy is acquired by holding firmly to the fact that "compartmentalization" is present in India, as in the rest of the world. The term is not felicitous, but the concept it stands for makes possible personal identity, the existence of objects, and even a proper religious experience.

Illusion, however, remains a conventional danger. Forster has created another contrapuntal arrangement. Even as he introduces the idea that reality requires limits, if it is not to threaten its own meaning and existence, he retains the common view that illusion menaces reality.

But illusion assumes many guises new to Forster's fictional world. The chief of these are "misunderstanding" and metaphysical seduction. Like Cathy at Heathcliff's window, they continually seek to enter the dwellings of reality and destroy them by imposing a deathly union on all that exists.

A prevalent source of misunderstanding is lack of self-knowledge, among Indians and English. Forster describes Aziz, "He was sensitive rather than responsive. In every remark he found a meaning, but not always the true meaning, and his life though vivid was largely a dream." [6] Fielding, too, despite his superiority to the other Englishmen and despite our sympathy with him, is not marked by self-knowledge deep enough to avert misunderstandings with others. Despite Forster's mild irony, his description of Fielding's difference from the other English, unattractive as they are, really indicates Fielding's lack of understanding of them. "He . . . did not realize that 'white' has no more to do with a colour than 'God save the King' with a god, and that it was the height of impropriety to consider what it does connote" (p. 66).

However, the central misunderstanding, from which most others eventually radiate, is the incident in the Marabar Caves. Adela's sensation of being attacked is not lightly dismissed by Forster, though Aziz is clearly innocent. If nothing else has happened to Adela, she has been threatened by the nothingness of the caves and the echo. Her hysteria is as much a fear of death and dissolution as it is the result of sexual repression. Misunderstanding and metaphysical seduction actually merge in this central episode.

The persistence of misunderstanding as a threat to reality becomes apparent after the trial, during which Adela recants, Aziz is vindicated, and the friendship between him and Fielding, who has never wavered in his belief in Aziz's innocence, seems strengthened. Moreover, both reaffirm their equation of friendship with love, a spirit that triumphs over misunderstanding.

But misunderstanding's readiness to weaken the fabric of a reality, in this case a friendship, defeats both men.

Aziz's compatriots discuss the compensation Adela ought to be forced to pay. Fielding, on the other hand, sympathizes with her and urges Aziz to settle for an apology.

The misunderstanding begins. Aziz "sees" that Fielding wants him to spare Adela "so that the English may say, 'Here is a native who has actually behaved like a gentleman; if it was not for his black face we would almost allow him to join our club' " (*p. 261*). Later, the argument over Adela persisting, Forster writes, "Aziz had no sense of evidence. The sequence of his emotions decided his beliefs, and led to the tragic coolness between himself and his English friend" (*p. 282*). In still another debate over the question of compensation, the remnant of the public school boy in Fielding is exasperated. He impulsively calls Aziz a "little rotter" (*p. 284*). Fielding immediately apologizes and insists that so slight a damage to their friendship should be erased. But "tangles like this still interrupted their intercourse. A pause in the wrong place, an intonation misunderstood, and a whole conversation went awry" (*p. 285*).

If friendship, the highest form of love, the best of personal relations, cannot endure, the message of A *Passage to India* may seem to be the echo Mrs. Moore hears in the Marabar Caves, the echo intimating that everything—from love to filth—is the same, and that nothing has reality. But another conclusion is also possible. The Western concept, "compartmentalization," challenges the void. Forster has written, "For the purpose of living one has to assume that the personality is solid, and the 'self' is an entity, and to ignore all contrary evidence." [7]

In A *Passage to India*, "person" appears to have replaced, in the interest of reality, even personal relations, as the highest good attainable. There is an inevitable link between "person" and compartmentalization.

For all his failures in personal relationships, Aziz remains, from the beginning to the end of the novel, a person. Forster has told us, "Aziz is modeled on Masood, my greatest Indian friend. . . . But I think of . . . Aziz . . . as [a person] and not as [a] religious [type]." [8]

Instructive also is what Forster imagines about the Emperor Babur who, in the novel, is Aziz's favorite Moslem hero. "But what a happiness to have known Babur! He had all that one seeks in a friend. His energy and ambition were touched with sensitiveness; he could act, feel, observe, and remember; though not critical of his senses, he was aware of their workings, thus fulfilling the whole nature of man." [9] In that last phrase—"the whole nature of man," and in the previous reference to Aziz as a "person" and not a "type," we glimpse a part of Forster's mind that was to work against the force of the echo in A *Passage to India.*

Various critics have amplified the importance of the individual to Forster and thus, by inference, of Aziz's identity. Arnold Kettle has said, "A writer who can say of himself that he is what his age and upbringing have made him is unlikely to fall into the barren error of regarding a human personality as outside time and place." [10] Santha Rama Rau, who dramatized A *Passage to India,* has observed, "[Forster] writes about individuals and their position in 'the human predicament,' gallantly keeping them individuals. . . ." [11] And in an early review of A *Passage to India,* J. B. Priestley concluded, "Everyone is treated as real persons should be treated—with a certain detached sympathy that is the very height of human justice." [12]

In a moonlit scene within a mosque, Forster early establishes Aziz's identity, "the ninety-nine names of God on the frieze stood out . . . against the sky. The contest between this dualism . . . pleased Aziz, and he tried to symbolize the whole into some truth of religion or love. . . . Here was Islam, his own country . . . an attitude towards life both exquisite and durable, where his body and his thoughts found their home" (*p. 21*).

Symbolic intention need not be claimed. Aziz himself is "exquisite and durable" and his thoughts at least do have a home in a country filled with the homeless.

His identity—selfhood—survives even the trial and the break-up of friendship with Fielding, Aziz's last attempt at "personal relations" with Europeans. Before communication between Aziz and Fielding ends (and they both leave

Chandrapore) Fielding succeeds in getting Aziz not to press Adela for compensation. Fielding triumphs in this instance by finally invoking the name of Mrs. Moore. During the scene in the mosque, she and Aziz had met, and he had loved her, worshipped her, ever since.

The question of Adela and compensation settled, much to the dissatisfaction of Aziz's Indian friends; Hamidullah, one of them, tells Aziz that he will remain a poor man, that his only course will be to "educate your children, read the latest scientific periodicals, compel European doctors to respect you. Accept the consequences of your own actions like a man." Aziz replies, "There are many ways of being a man; mine is to express what is deepest in my heart" (*p. 280*). What is deepest in his heart is the reverential memory of Mrs. Moore. She, to whom so many meanings have been ascribed, is thus responsible for one instance of Aziz's assertion of identity.

When error upon error has destroyed the possibility of friendship between Fielding and Aziz, Forster, near the end of the novel, uses their reunion not so much to redeem the past as to push against obstacles, in order to reconfirm Aziz's selfhood. Aziz is forced to acknowledge another misunderstanding: that Fielding's wife is Stella, Mrs. Moore's daughter, not Adela Quested. He is forced to realize that the misunderstanding has been deepened by the conniving of his relative, Mahmoud Ali (who has read Fielding's letters, after the Englishman returns to England, and has encouraged Aziz, who has refused to look at them, in his delusion). But he angrily repudiates Fielding and says that he forgives Mahmoud Ali "because he loved me." And Forster writes of Aziz, "He had built his life on a mistake, but he had built it" (*p. 315*).

As for Fielding, his personal identity is almost emblematic. He is a man of ideas. He is as free of racial bias as anyone, according to Forster, can be. He continually alienates himself from the English in Chandrapore. He completes the process when the English community gathers in its club, out of fear of the Indians and out of a sense of solidarity. Fielding takes this inopportune moment to reiterate his defense of Aziz. Indignant exchanges follow, and Fielding resigns from the club. His action is a formality; he would have been expelled.

At another time, in conversation with Aziz, he makes explicit his credo, and thus his sense of himself. "I believe in teaching people to be individuals, and to understand other individuals. It's the only thing I do believe in" (pp. 126–27). F. C. Crews notes "the refusal to abandon personality, which is the strongest bond between Aziz and the Westerners. . . ." [13]

When Fielding has left India and rediscovered in Venice his Western sense of reality, he reflects, "without form, how can there be beauty?" (p. 293). His feeling for form, reawakened in the Mediterranean world, would be impossible without a sense of personal identity.

There is also "personality" or "identity" in what he says to Adela, shortly before both leave India. Telling her that he does not believe in heaven, he adds, "Yet I believe that honesty gets us there" (p. 249). Quixotically, Fielding has provided two of Forster's coordinates for personality: rationalism and honesty.

About the mystical Mrs. Moore, her experience in the cave, her influence upon people and events long after she has departed India and died, much has and can be said. In need of emphasis, however, are the rational limits within which Forster has enclosed her and within which she, too, appears as a "person." On the train carrying the English and Indians to the Marabar Caves, her mood and sensibility are jolted just as much as they will be when she will hear later the nihilistic echo within the cave. "She felt increasingly (vision or nightmare?) that, though people are important, the relations between them are not" (p. 141).

Of her experience within the cave, F. C. Crews has observed, "Instead of blending her identity with that of the world-soul, she reduces the world-soul to the scale of her . . . own ego; her dilettantish yearning for oneness with the universe has been echoed, not answered." [14] It is not his main object, but Crews has called attention to the fact that Mrs. Moore, so often discussed as a disembodied mystical spirit, is also recognizable and definable by a Western and rationally limiting term, ego.

It can be argued that Adela is or is not a "person" before her ordeal at the trial, but Forster intends her to emerge, from the courtroom, as one—within her limits. Describing her in a conversation with Fielding, after the trial, Forster writes, "Although her hard school-mistressy manner remained, she was no longer examining life but being examined by it; she had become a real person" (*p.* 254).

Objects, too, have identity that challenges the nothingness implicit in the echo of the Marabar Caves. Wasps, stones, temples, mosques do exist. The most telling defiance of the void by objects occurs during Mrs. Moore's leave-taking of India and, later Fielding's.

As Mrs. Moore approaches and reaches Bombay, Forster writes,

> She watched the indestructible life of man and his changing faces, and the houses he has built for himself and God. . . . There was, for instance, a place called Asirgarh . . . an enormous fortress among wooded hills. . . . it had huge and noble bastions and to the right of them was a mosque. . . . it seemed to say: 'I do not vanish.' . . . thousands of coco-nut palms appeared all around the anchorage and climbed the hills to wave her farewell. 'So you thought an echo was India; you took the Marabar caves as final?' they laughed. 'What have we in common with them, or they with Asirgarh? Good-bye!' (*pp.* 218–19).

Emphasizing the matter somewhat differently, Alan Wilde has written, "The passages describing Mrs. Moore's trip . . . constitute the turning point of the novel: in them is intimated Forster's counterstatement to the message of the Marabar. . . . But it is . . . wrong . . . to assume that the vision of the caves is cancelled. Mrs. Moore was . . . not wrong in what she saw . . . wrong not in assuming that beneath all man's efforts there lies an abyss, but in refusing to go on despite (but not ignoring) the fact." [15] Had she "gone on," she might not have been mocked by the call of separate identity at her leave-taking.

Fielding's departure from India also reasserts the moral and concrete essence of things, but on a world scale wider than the one implicit in the description of Mrs. Moore's leave-taking. As Fielding, on his way home, stops briefly in Italy, Forster writes, "The Mediterranean is the human norm. When men leave that exquisite lake, whether through the Bosphorus or the Pillars of Hercules, they approach the monstrous and extraordinary; and the southern exit leads to the strangest experience of all. Turning his back on it yet again, [Fielding] took the train northward, and tender romantic fancies that he thought were dead forever, flowered when he saw the buttercups and daisies of June" (*p. 293*). Forster has reasserted here not only the real division of Fielding's world—India, the Mediterranean, and England—but has even challenged the unreality of India's echo with the reality of the most fragile of things—"the buttercups and daisies of June."

Finally, however, compartmentalization—in all its manifestations the philosophic ground for affirming concrete reality—is a good-and-evil that always strives to conquer the evil. It cannot and should not completely succeed, for to do so would be to eliminate part of man's personality.

Part III, "Temple," examines man's effort to remove the evil through religion. However, there are many previous indications of what the possibilities for achieving this quest are; there are also indications of the danger, inherent in the quest, to the humanistic connotations of "compartmentalization."

The idea of unity helps characterize many of the participants in the story, just as the idea gives form and meaning to the novel as a whole. Two characters with whom the idea is consistently associated are Mrs. Moore and Professor Godbole.

Early in the novel, Mrs. Moore has her first sensation of unity.

> Mrs. Moore, whom the club had stupified, woke up outside. She watched the moon, whose radiance stained with primrose the purple of the surrounding sky. In Eng-

land the moon had seemed dead and alien; here she was caught in the shawl of night together with earth and all the other stars. A sudden sense of unity, of kinship with the heavenly bodies, passed into the old woman and out, like water through a tank, leaving a strange freshness behind (*p. 32*).

Her experience of unity is real enough—it revives her—but the image of water passing through a tank suggests also that illusion has subtly disguised itself and become attached to reality. The ou-boum of the caves has been anticipated.

Another important moment is her noticing a wasp hanging from her clothing peg. " 'Pretty dear,' said Mrs. Moore to the wasp. He did not wake, but her voice floated out, to swell the night's uneasiness" (*p. 38*). The wasp will reappear during Professor Godbole's religious striving, in Part III, but it will then and there be associated with the limits imposed upon humans in their attempts to love infinitely, just as Mrs. Moore's voice, joining the unity of the all-embracing night, only increases its uneasiness. The difference between Godbole's later embrace of the wasp and Mrs. Moore's attempt at affection for it becomes, in retrospect, another comment upon unity.

Mrs. Moore does have a rational insight into the limits of unity—of God and transcendental love. She says, "God . . . is . . . love," a definition that will recur, distorted in spelling by the Hindus, in Part III. She continues, "The desire to behave pleasantly satisfies God . . . The sincere if impotent desire wins His blessing. I think everyone fails, but there are so many kinds of failure" (*p. 55*).

This is the high point of her rationalistic religion. Henceforth, the influence of a unity implicitly evil and antagonistic will lead to her weakening and dissolution.

Professor Godbole parallels her but is more complex. He, too, aspires to an all-inclusive love, and fails. Unlike Mrs. Moore, however, he is redeemed in failure: he experiences happiness. Early in the novel, he sings a song. Concluding it, he says, "I will explain . . . It was a religious song. I placed myself in the position of a milkmaiden. I say to Shri Krishna, 'Come! come to me only.' The god refuses to come. I grow humble. . . . 'Do not come to me only. Multiply yourself into a hundred Krishnas, and let one go to each of my hundred companions, but one, O Lord of the Universe, come to me.' He refuses to come."

Mrs. Moore, who is present, asks gently, "But He comes in some other song, I hope?" Godbole answers, "Oh, no, he refuses to come. . . . I say to Him, 'Come, come, come, come, come, come.' He neglects to come." (*p. 84*). Godbole understands—more, at least, than does Mrs. Moore. "*Come, come:* the repetition of the word occurs throughout the novel and serves as one of the rhythmic devices. To Godbole, union with God is always a desire, not a reality; as the [subsequent] Marabar incident [indicates], to achieve Him would inevitably mark the end of love." [16]

During the religious rites in Mau, in Part III, which begins two years after the trial of Aziz, the precise nature of Godbole's religious aspiration and experience becomes dramatically clear.

Professor Narayan Godbole stands in the presence of God. God is not born yet . . . but He has also been born centuries ago, nor can He ever be born, because He is the Lord of the Universe, who transcends human processes. He is, was not, is not, was. He and Professor Godbole stood at opposite ends of the same strip of carpet (*p. 295*).

In the midst of muddle, confusion, and merriment, the Professor dances. The dance itself is religion. Godbole

. . . loved all men, the whole universe, and scraps of their past, tiny splinters of detail, emerged for a moment to melt into the universal warmth. . . . though she was not important to him, [Godbole] remembered an old woman he had met in Chandrapore. . . . and he impelled her by his spiritual force to that place where completeness can be found. Completeness, not reconstruction. His senses grew thinner, he remembered a wasp seen he forgot where, perhaps on a stone. He loved the wasp equally, he impelled it like-wise, he was imitating God. And the stone where the wasp clung—could he . . . no, he could not, he had been wrong to attempt the stone, logic and conscious effort had seduced, he came back to the strip of red carpet and discovered that he was dancing upon it (*p.* 298).

Godbole cannot imitate God—should not, because in *Passage* really successful imitation might as easily lead to vision of the meaningless void as to a vision of all-embracing love. But the effort must be made, precisely because it will fail. The conclusion of the rite resolves the paradox.

> Professor Godbole had once more developed the life of his spirit. He had . . . again seen Mrs. Moore. . . . It was his duty, as it was his desire, to place himself in the position of the God and to love her. . . . How inadequate! But each according to his own capacities, and he knew that his own were small. "One old Englishwoman and one little, little wasp," he thought. . . . "It does not seem much, still it is more than I am myself." (*pp.* 302–3).

Only partial self-transcendance has occurred. But it is happiness, signified by dancing, and has enabled Godbole to go beyond his ordinary capacity for love and awareness. His achievement brings us back to one of the meanings of "compartments" in the novel: to the experience of self—and self at its realistic best.

The parallel between Mrs. Moore, at her own high moment, and Godbole, here, is important. Hugh Maclean, referring to one of the painted signs that are part of the rites, links the characters. "On one [sign] is the legend 'God si Love.' In English to demonstrate God's universality, its error shows only that the desire serves for the deed, which, as most Westerners do not see, is of little account. Failure in this sense is and must be integral to life. And yet, as Mrs. Moore had observed, 'I think everyone fails, but there are so many kinds of failure.' " [17] Had this been Mrs. Moore's sustained conviction in the novel, she, like Godbole, would have been an affirmation of the degree of unthreatening unity possible in this world. She would have known that the effort to transcend self guarantees the existence of self. She would not have been defeated by the echo of the caves.

There is a link between Forster's approval of the limited

self and his acceptance, without despair, of division. The barrier between the limited self and the one it aspires to be, resembles the obstacle between individuals who try to love each other. Thus, Godbole, Fielding, and Aziz are related through their different but analogous experiences, though Godbole and Aziz understand their true positions better than Fielding does his.

James McConkey has touched tangentially on the subject. "Forster seems to be saying . . . that human relations seem ever strengthened through division," and, "the Hindu division of realities—a division which, while affirming the existence of an absolute, makes its approach impossible to conscious man—offers a parallel to Forster's own philosophical view." [18] McConkey has stressed human relations rather than personality. But had he added that Aziz's assertion of self is also part of Forster's view, McConkey might have linked all three central characters of "Temple."

As the novel draws to a close, Forster reiterates his warning against the possibly nihilistic meaning of unity. He does so through a continuing series of divisions, each expressing itself as the necessary ground for existence and reality in this world.

During the festival celebrating the birth of Krishna a religious float, a boat carrying Fielding and his wife, and another boat with Aziz and Ralph aboard collide. The collision is accompanied by thunder, a warning that the effort to unite must end in collision rather than merger if the echo of the caves is not to triumph over life.

The scene serves also as background for Aziz and Fielding's final meeting. The two men are riding together on horseback. Fielding intends a full reconciliation. But Aziz excitedly talks politics. "India shall be a nation! No foreigners of any sort! Hindu and Moslem and Sikh and all shall be one. . . ."

Fielding mockingly regards the outburst as nineteenth-century nationalism, "and Aziz in an awful rage danced this way and that . . . and cried: 'Down with the English anyhow. That is certain. . . . We may hate

one another, but we hate you most . . . if it's fifty-five
hundred years we shall get rid of you . . . and then,' he
concluded, half kissing him, 'you and I shall be friends.' "

Fielding is confused. " 'Why can't we be friends now?'
. . . [he said] . . . holding him affectionately. 'It's what I
want. It's what you want.' "

Forster concludes the novel, "But the horses didn't
want it—they swerved apart; the earth didn't want it,
sending up rocks through which riders must pass single
file; the temples, the tank, the jail, the palace, the birds,
the carrion, the Guest House, that came into view as they
issued from the gap and saw Mau beneath: they didn't
want it, they said in their hundred voices, 'No, not yet,'
and the sky said, 'No, not there' " (*pp.* 335–36).

Speaking in their full voice, at the strategic conclusion
of the novel, are the associated objects and values dependent for existence upon the structural force and boundaries
of compartmentalization. Not only do objects assert their
identity but the horses swerving apart, and the rocks,
permitting only single file passage, place personality above
"personal relations."

Forster has resisted the metaphysical seduction into
nothingness of the caves. Through characterization, he
has also created a moral imperative to resist. Compartmentalization is a Western concept. We might have expected Fielding to be its chief spokesman. Yet it is Godbole, the alleged mystic; and Aziz, the victim of a hundred
self-created misunderstandings; who assert the doctrine
and hold to it. Fielding, in fact, is barely rescued by Aziz
from Mrs. Moore's error and fate.

The conclusion of the novel tells us that time and space
are the coordinates of all phenomena, of the material
universe and of the love it can support. Fielding's perfect
friendship, if achieved, would require the obliteration of
these coordinates, of the world they generate and hold
together. The apparent hostility to his wish, of the universe, of its substance and attitude, is in fact kindness to
Fielding.

Aziz has relearnt what he knew at the beginning of the

novel and had forgotten in Part II. His symbolic "half-kiss" is the degree of love possible if identity is to survive in the presence of the opposing pull of politics, race, and the void. It is the degree of love attained by Godbole, who could propel toward himself Mrs. Moore and the wasp but not the stone. Fielding's "affectionate embrace," by contrast, is the muddled echo of the caves, an ingenuous flirtation with the danger of nothingness.

In the last scene of the novel, the real—the phenomenal and the psychological—has contended with the unreal—a universe devoid of time and space. But knowing the danger with which it tempts man, the universe itself—the sky and the earth—saves the day. By keeping Fielding and Aziz apart, it preserves their existence. And since Aziz knows the conditions of reality, the universe permits him to instruct Fielding and even to reward his effort at friendship. Aziz, in granting the half-kiss, is entitled to say, with Professor Godbole, "It does not seem much, still it is more than I am myself." If Fielding has learnt from Aziz, A *Passage to India* ends affirmatively. It says that imperfect affection, replacing an illusory one that has necessarily been destroyed, shores up the reality of the world.

AT CAMBRIDGE, Forster read history and classics for his degree. He has made his enduring mark as a novelist, of course, but both before and after he stopped publishing novels, he wrote essays touching on literature, the past, and contemporary political and social events. For the most part, his style and tone do not vary—regardless of the subject at hand. As V. S. Pritchett has observed, Forster has always refused to speak in a public voice.[1]

This refusal thwarts any effort to distinguish neatly the divisions of his aesthetic, moral, and social interests. On some subjects, he deliberately avoids the role of expert. Writing about matters with which he is well acquainted, he never (for the purpose of some allegedly objective truth) sacrifices the casual, personal note.

Yet, without distorting his temperament and outlook, his work—excluding the novels—can be divided into categories, so long as it is recognized that not everything will fit conveniently into one division or another. Forster, himself, despite his refusal to create sharp boundaries among matters of aesthetic, intellectual, and moral concern, has grouped and defined his expository writings.

Alexandria: A Guide, first published in 1922, is a history of Alexandria and a related topographical description of the city. *Pharos and Pharillon* (1923) is another study of Alexandria, "Pharos, the vast and heroic lighthouse that dominated the first city—under Pharos I have grouped a few antique events; to modern events and to personal impressions I have given the name of Pharillon, the obscure successor of Pharos." [2]

In 1927, when Forster published his Clark lectures as *Aspects of the Novel,* he confirmed his right to the mantle of literary critic. His biography of Goldsworthy Lowes Dickenson (1934) suggests a new category of interest. And when Forster, in 1936, put together a collection of his essays—*Abinger Harvest*—he arranged the included pieces in groups: "The Present," [3] "Books," "The Past," and "The East." He concluded the volume with his pageant play, "The Abinger Pageant," and thus rounded the volume off with a return to the fictional, or dramatic.

In his postwar publications, Forster has continued the easy eclecticism that has always marked his expository writing. *Two Cheers for Democracy* (1951) is a second collection of essays, and like *Abinger Harvest,* is arranged in sections: "The Second Darkness" and "What I Believe." The second part is subdivided into "Art in General," "The Arts in Action," and "Places." His next book, *The Hill of Devi* (1953), is largely a collection of letters written home during his two early visits to India. It is now, because of particular episodes described, a source book for *Passage.* But in full scope, it is a deceptive one. It dwells on life in the household of a native ruler, a minor detail of Part III of *Passage.* Nevertheless, it provides, as suggested earlier, service. It helps explain why Forster, in India, could not continue work on *Passage. The Hill of Devi* consists of raw impressions. Furthermore, if Forster's self-described position is not a false one, the reason is that his charm, curiosity, and tolerant responsiveness to the different and the chaotic enabled him to accommodate himself to his role.

But the energy required by this performance displaced the drive to write. The half-soporific, half-hysterical atmosphere of the palace in Mau defeated intellect and controlled imagination. It beckoned to formlessness, Forster's nemesis as a writer and the metaphysical evil of *Passage.* Once back in England, the narrowing of the gap between India remembered and experienced was in part a repudiation of Mau. *The Hill of Devi* would be enriched by an introduction or epilogue discussing its more subtle relation to *Passage*.

Forster's most recent book, *Marianne Thornton* (1956) concerns a relative but recalls *Goldsworthy Lowes Dickenson*. Both biographies place their subjects in an historical era and are casually overlaid with avowals and digressions expressing Forster's own values. *Marianne Thornton,* then, is further demonstration of his disinclination to speak in a public voice. Whether the particular quality of his private voice is suited to the drama of biography is dubious, a fact evident also in *Goldsworthy Lowes Dickenson*. Whether the Forsterian tone and manner interfere, in the writing of biography, with providing information is even more debatable. No doubt from a literal viewpoint they do. But Forster surprises. For long stretches, he can be so detailed and monotoned that he seems to be parodying the worst kind of biographical writing. Then, too, solipsism, periodically dominant in *Marianne Thornton,* is for the expert reader a source of information even about the book's putative subject. Finally, in the later pages of *Marianne Thornton* Forster is born and depicted in childhood. Curiously, however, the explicitly autobiographical passages supply the same pleasure and require the same search for meaning, an invasion of the aura surrounding them, as does the rest of the book.

To bring together Forster's expository writing, two guiding principles are required. The largest categories should be employed, and despite this liberal arrangement individual pieces must be expected to cross boundaries. These caveats accepted, the largest and most natural divisions reveal themselves as discussions of literature, the past, and the present.[4]

There is no all-logical reason for beginning with Forster as literary critic. Some of his early essays on the past and present are contemporary with the publication of his fiction and of his initial literary criticism. There is, however, a semilogical reason for the procedure. Although Forster's career as a publishing novelist ended in 1924 with *Passage,* nineteen years after his first novel appeared, his reputation is still based largely on his fiction. A critically impure curiosity—Forster inspires it—is therefore to want to know, immediately after we have read the novels, what he has written about literature.

Central in a discussion of Forster as literary critic or theoretician is *Aspects of the Novel* (1927). Originally delivered in Cambridge as the Clark lectures, the chapters are, to a degree, casual and colloquial. And in 1927, Forster, the master of surface presentation who will never let surfaces alone, provides another reason for our proceeding from his career as a writer of fiction to his practice of literary criticism. Defending his refusal to make major alterations for publication of the lectures, he adds, "and . . . since the novel is itself often colloquial it may possibly withhold some of its secrets from the graver and grander streams of criticism, and may reveal them to backwaters and shallows." [5]

However, if we permit his apologetics to disarm us completely, we shall miss the illumination of literary theory and the practice of criticism marking the most significant parts of *Aspects.* These sections try to confront the challenge facing any sophisticated humanist, what is the relation between literature and daily life? Forster's answers, furthermore, attempt to convert themselves into practical critical principles.

The novel is approached through seven aspects: "The Story," "People," "The Plot," "Fantasy," "Prophecy," "Pattern," and "Rhythm." [6] Forster immediately throws down, gentlemanly nonbelligerent, the gauntlet to the many belligerent schools of criticism flourishing in the '20's.

Any definition of the novel, he maintains, must be broad and liberal enough to include such extreme variants as *The Pilgrim's Progress* and Joyce's *Ulysses.* Recent abandonments of critical fortresses, as well as the decision of more independent men that the mandarins of criticism, however influential, should leave ground to roam, have revived Forster's point of view. [7]

As *Aspects* progresses, Forster moves from the most concrete attributes of the novel to the most abstruse—the most difficult to discuss. The fact in itself should dispel any misguided thoughts about the book's intention. In writing it, or rather in composing the lectures, he not only carefully planned his approach but apportioned his intellectual energy in accordance with the relative difficulties of the sequence of challenges he set himself.

His definition of story seems innocuous enough, but what this simple concept reflects is a decision to begin by anchoring his discussion in something unassailable: "[Story] is a narrative of events arranged in their time sequence," and appeals to the primitive in us: our desire to know what happens next (*AN, p. 29*). In Forster's sense, the lack of sequence among the scenes of much contemporary drama and narrative obliterates story. Were a debate arranged between Forster and more recent, experimental authors, the obliteration would be precisely the point argued.

Not the least of the changes that have occurred in fiction since World War II have been new attitudes toward time. They range from serious attempts to reconstruct our sense of it to expulsions of its presence from narrative. Forster is actually less concerned about the time-sense, in his definition of story, than are many modern writers about their nihilist philosophies of time in fiction; yet he would no sooner reject time from the novel than he would exclude other aspects.

When he proceeds to these other aspects, he begins in earnest his effort to relate clearly daily life and art. Besides time, there seems something else in life, " 'value,' . . . which is measured . . . by intensity, so that when we look at our past it . . . piles up into a few notable pinnacles, and when we look at the future it . . . never seems a chronological chart. . . . So daily life . . . is . . . composed of two lives—the life in time and the life by values—and our conduct reveals a double allegiance. . . . And . . . the entire novel . . . [includes] the life by values as well" (*AN, pp. 29–30*).

The link established between life and the novel, whatever Forster's ultimate intention, is thus close and intimate. But he has not reconciled life and art; he has entangled them. Although he has not done so in a manner alien to his humanism, he has made it difficult to establish a true theoretical reconciliation between the two.

The entanglement continues. Forster's second aspect of the novel is called "People" rather than characters. Surprisingly, however, under a rubric so critically unpromising, technical considerations casually enter and depart, although we would be hard put to detect each time they appear and then slip away. We can, however, illustrate, through an instance, how Forster does occasionally make "People" a true critical idea. Discussing this second of his aspects of the novel, he says, "the novelist will . . . [appeal] to our intelligence and imagination, not merely to our curiosity. A new emphasis enters his voice: emphasis upon value" (AN, *p. 43*).

However, even this observation is mixed in intention and effect. Although it is a critical concept, it is equally, and perhaps even more so, a reminder that any technical process serves for Forster a larger human interest: the necessity in art of moral values. His equal or primary concern with this nontechnical matter is confirmed by what he immediately adds. "Since the novelist is himself a human being, there is an affinity between him and his subject-matter which is absent in many other forms of art" (AN, *pp. 43–44*).

There is, however, a viewpoint that rescues Forster from appearing too casual about technique, or from seeming to consider it in only sporadic intervals. He has not, after all, avoided the subject. His allusions to technique can be viewed as invitations to the reader to work out for himself the full critical implications of Forster's passing references to method. The reader can isolate Forster's glances at technique from the purposes Forster himself insists on attaching to it.

Thus, when he says that there is an affinity between the novelist and his subject matter, we can develop the implications. The "affinity" is an early stage in the creative process. Life is raw and formless, and the good novelist experiences it as such.

An analogy is a sculptor's approach to wood, stone, marble, or granite. The process is "technical," but without intimate knowledge of the raw material the sculptor would be unable to elicit form from it. So, too, according to Forster, the novelist, because he is a human being, acquires, if less deliberately, an intimate knowledge of his own particular formless material—life. And like the sculptor, he will fashion his material to his own ends.

Aspects of the Novel also contains, however, detailed confrontations of technical problems, although these undulate—one is tempted to say rhythmically—with discursive stretches that are only allusively technical, or are simply, in emphasis, expressions of Forster's humanism.

The most sustained critical effort in the chapter on "People" begins with an observation by Alain, "All that is observable in a man . . . his actions and such of his spiritual existence as can be deduced from [them]—falls into the domain of history. But his . . . romantic side . . . the dreams, joys, sorrows, and self-communings which politeness or shame prevent him from mentioning [are expressed in the novel]" (AN, *pp.* 45–46).

Alain inspires Forster to a clear and applicable critical distinction between people in daily life and in books: "In daily life . . . we know each other approximately, by external signs, and these serve well enough as a basis for society and even for intimacy. But people in a novel can be understood completely . . . if the novelist wishes . . . they do not contain any secrets, whereas our friends do and must, mutual secrecy being one of the conditions of life upon this globe" (AN, *pp.* 46–47).

Reading these words, we discern a concrete principle for analyzing the novel. But we also feel an impulse encouraged by Forster's own practice—not here—but in many parts of *Aspects of the Novel,* to enlarge our perception of an analytical device into an exploration of its broad humanistic implications. Thus we reflect that every period has its cultural illusions and that one of ours, today, is that in daily life many of the secrets Forster had in mind are now bared.

In fairness to him, however, we should add that through historical change we have learnt something. In its most recently assigned meaning, a "secret" signifies not the kind most readily called up by the word in 1927 but inarticulateness and lack of insight. These, now, afflict the man in daily life. If he does not deliberately conceal much of what is alluded to by Forster, the new or newly discovered privacies behind surface incoherence or blankness have become increasingly important in our literary perspective. If the novelist wishes to disclose the "secrets" of his character his formal task remains similar to Alain's and Forster's summation. Another surviving aspect of Forster's discussion (of the novelist's ability to reveal secrets) is that it anticipates his subsequent definition of a "round" character (AN, pp. 65–75 passim,) a technical term that has itself remained useful for the description of characters in some of the fiction written since Forster conceived the idea.

But the first concept in *Aspects of the Novel* that completely differentiates fiction from life is "plot." It is no accident that Forster analyses plot firmly and resourcefully and that his own best novels, even when characters shape the plot, turn on its intellectual energy, its moral purpose, and its emerging form. Nor is there any anomaly in Forster's concluding an unsympathetic critique of Meredith by noting, "And yet he is in one way a great novelist. He is the finest contriver that English fiction has ever produced, and any lecture on plot must do homage to him" (AN, p. 86).

Forster's tone, in his discussion of plot, is matter-of-fact, "A plot [like a story] is also a narrative of events," but "the emphasis [falls] on causality" (AN, p. 82). However, Forster insists that apprehension of plot requires memory and intelligence.

In themselves, these can again be regarded as pertaining to daily life. But in their active engagement with a novel, memory and intelligence have, according to Forster, a special function. They will look for something other than the time process, values, or people. They will engage in a more abstract and difficult enterprise: a search for connections, a constant review of the position of details in relation to each other, and an ultimate effort to discern, retrospectively, the total form.

There is a similarity between Forster's discussion of plot and its consideration by Percy Lubbock, whose *Craft of Fiction* (1921) has often been compared, as a formal treatment of its subject, with *Aspects of the Novel* (to the disadvantage of the latter). There is also a suggestive parallel between Forster's conception of plot and G. M. Hopkins' "inscape," although this engaging possibility is ultimately cancelled by the different conditions for apprehension established by Forster and Hopkins. Forster's requirements exclude all humanistic and spiritual concerns, even his own. "The intelligent novel-reader . . . mentally picks up [a new fact]. He sees it from two points of view: isolated, and related to other facts that he has read on previous pages" (AN, *pp.* 83–84). As for memory, it is closely connected with intelligence, "for unless we remember we cannot understand" (*p.* 84).

Forster's discussion of plot consistently separates art from life—a fact already noted. To human faculties he has assigned a function exclusively devoted to comprehension of the nonhuman. As the plot unfolds, "over it . . . will hover the memory of the reader (that dull glow of the mind of which intelligence is the bright advancing edge) and will constantly rearrange and reconsider, seeing new clues, new chains of cause and effect, and the final sense . . . will not be of clues or chains, but of something aesthetically compact. . . . We come up against beauty here—for the first time in our inquiry" (AN, *pp.* 84–85). Like plot, beauty distinguishes art from life.

However, Forster's treatment of his next aspect of the novel, "fantasy," again blurs the distinction between art and life—or people. But Forster approaches his subject as he did the affinity between a novelist and his work, so that we are again encouraged to develop for ourselves the purely critical concept inherent in his discourse.

This time Forster associates the reader rather than the writer with the novel, "What does fantasy ask of us? . . . It compels us to an adjustment . . . different [from the one] required by a work of art, to an additional adjustment. The other novelists say, 'Here is something that might occur in your lives,' the fantasist, 'Here is something that could not occur' " (*AN*, *p. 101*).

Forster's fantasies were not novels but short stories, and an outsider's viewpoint is apparent in his discussion of fantasy. But from that viewpoint art and a human being—the reader—are again linked. And the human in this case is really a particular man: E. M. Forster.

Nevertheless, the technical implication is accessible to us. Because the fantasist asks us to accept something that could not occur in our lives, he requires of us a sophisticated literary imagination. Although this imagination is derived from a general human faculty, in relation to the novel it functions (according to Forster's suggestive remarks) like memory and intelligence for a special end— perception of a purely literary phenomenon, and for the latter's own sake. Perception of fantasy, in this unique situation, is for an abstractly aesthetic purpose, not a humanistic or spiritual one.

"Prophecy" is an even more important aspect of the novel than is "fantasy." In at least three novels, *A Room with a View*, *Howards End*, and *A Passage to India*, Forster's own prophetic impulse plays a part in shaping the whole. His definition of prophecy is therefore of three-fold interest. It throws light on his own novelistic practice, it further reveals his taste in reading, and it continues the empirical theory of the novel he is developing: "Prophecy—in our sense—is a tone of voice. . . . We shall have to attend to the novelist's state of mind and to the actual words he uses; we shall neglect as far as we can the problems of common sense" (*AN*, *pp. 116–17*).

Prophecy is further characterized and distinguished from fantasy. "Prophetic fiction, then, seems to have definite characteristics. It demands humility and the absence of a sense of humour. It reaches back. . . . It is spasmodically realistic. And it gives us the sensation of a song or of sound. It is unlike fantasy because its face is toward unity, whereas fantasy glances about. Its confusion is incidental, whereas fantasy's is fundamental (*AN, p. 126*).

A question about "unity" in *Passage* occurs. Forster's admiration, in 1927, for prophetic fiction would raise no problems had he not identified such writing with "unity." But since he has, he apparently changed, in some quarter of his outlook, during the three years separating *Passage* from *Aspects of the Novel*.

But perhaps he has never placed himself among writers gifted with true visionary power. Perhaps he believes they would have seen *through* the Marabar echo to something affirmative. In 1927 *Passage* was probably still vivid to him. Did Forster, temperamentally wedded to humanism, defer, in *Aspects* to writers who he believed had an authentic prophetic ability?

Whatever the answer, his treatment of prophecy is, stylistically, a high mark in *Aspects*. As an analytic principle, "prophecy" may be less critically useful, even less possible of development by the reader himself, than are other aspects of the novel discussed by Forster. The ultimate inference is that he turned from critic and theoretician to reporter. The result is unfortunate. Many of the attributes Forster ascribes to prophetic fiction actually are present in his own work. If he had hit upon a nonmetaphorical equivalent for "its face is turned toward unity" he might not only have been inferentially consistent. He might have developed "prophecy" into a true critical principle. But the change would have required a tonal shift in one of the best written sections of *Aspects*, and more might have been lost than gained.

Pattern and Rhythm are two of Forster's aspects most applicable for critical purposes, perhaps because both effectively structure his own novels. To Forster, pattern is the less important of the two. He sees it as pictorial—an over-all image—and suspects that writers like Henry James sacrifice too much of the "person" for pattern. He does not recall that he himself partially, on occasion, sacrificed "people" to "pattern," specifically at the conclusions of *Where Angels Fear to Tread* and *The Longest Journey*. In fairness, however, it must be said that he usually does not make the sacrifice and that even in the instances mentioned his intention and extent are not Jamesian. Forster's feelings and viewpoint on the subject are emphatic and clear.

His discussion of rhythm raises no problems. "Rhythm is sometimes quite easy. Beethoven's Fifth Symphony, for instance, starts with the rhythm 'diddidy dum,' which we can all hear and tap to. But the symphony as a whole has also a rhythm—due mainly to the relation between its movements—which some people can hear but no one can tap to" (*AN, p. 151*).

One of Forster's examples of the first kind of rhythm is the repetition of "the 'little phrase' in the music of Vinteuil" that stitches "internally" *Rememberance of Things Past*. (*AN, p. 152*). But examples of the larger rhythm, Forster tells us, are not easily discernible. He might, however, have named *Passage*, built out of three rhythmically related blocks. As much as any other aspect, its rhythm creates this novel's stature.

Concluding *Aspects of the Novel*, we see in retrospect that Forster has only occasionally linked humanism and technique. We are also reminded that we must develop ourselves the critical principles in the suggestive leads to them he sometimes interposes. However, at the very end of *Aspects*, he once again puts aside "people" and "values." His strategy is to reconsider, through analogy, the beauty of form in a novel. He succeeds. "Music, though it does not employ human beings, though it is governed by intricate laws . . . [offers] in its final expression a type of beauty which fiction might achieve in its own way. Expansion. That is the idea the novelist must cling to. Not completion. Not rounding off but opening out" (*AN, p. 155*).

This dictum is both poetically suggestive and concrete.

It describes a quality, in the final pages of a work of fiction, discernible to anyone who has read widely in the novel. And though Forster's two best works, *Howards End* and *Passage*, end not with expansion but with the completion inherent in tableaux, the fact does not diminish the viability of his final insight in *Aspects*.

If *Aspects* is a clue, both common and uncommon sense suggest that Forster's entire career as a literary critic should be approached with tolerance—for our sake not his. As in *Aspects*, in his other essays we are often confronted by critical questions never answered. But again, as in *Aspects*, his literary essays, though never for long detaching themselves from humanism, surprise and delight with unexpected insights, practical and impractical, casting light on Forster and his own fiction, obscuring both in order to illuminate some corner hitherto deprived of adequate light; and modestly calling attention to what he himself could not accomplish in fiction.

"Joseph Conrad: A Note" (1920) is an example of two of these virtues. It is an illuminating glance at Conrad and a confession that in Forster's own novels a circumscribed dilemma is often the nearest approach to tragic truth, ". . . together with [his] loyalties and prejudices and personal scruples, he holds another ideal . . . a love of Truth. But Truth is a flower in whose neighbourhood others must wither, and Mr. Conrad has no intention that the blossoms he has culled with such pains and in so many lands should suffer and be thrown aside." [8]

The insight is excellent but prompts us to wonder how much aborted tragedy died in early drafts of Forster's novels because his wise instinct settled finally for what he could do naturally: create vivid scenes, write poetic prose, and achieve a whimsical or wry or ironic but never profoundly tragic tone.

This is not a subject to moralize upon. Moreover, Forster does in his novels touch tragedy, although he never reaches Conrad's depth of tragic exploration nor sustains over long intervals Conrad's penetrative power. Forster has been less free with his own "secrets" than has Conrad, and perhaps the fact explains partially Forster's inability to match Conrad's lifelong, tortured achievement as a writer of great tragedy. But it is equally appropriate simply to say that temperamental differences separate the two authors. Forster has never been inclined or able to permit the "truth," as he has perceived it and employed it thematically in his novels, to wither in the neighborhood of other blossoms, more important in literature though they may be.

In "The Early Novels of Virginia Woolf" (1925), Forster reveals an expected preference in a humanist—an attachment to the eighteenth- and nineteenth-century English novels. But he reveals also an early effort to resolve his restlessness about technique apparent in *Aspects*. In the smaller compass of the 1925 essay, however, the evidence is indirect. Without denying his humanist taste for the older novel form, he wishes to avoid the philistinism of simple nostalgia for the past and of rejection of the new and experimental. Thus, "the problem before [Virginia Woolf] . . . that would inaugurate a new literature if solved—is to retain her . . . new method and form, and yet allow her readers to inhabit each character with Victorian thoroughness" (*AH, p. 133*).

But to "inhabit a character with Victorian thoroughness" is to employ amply—and to subordinate interest in the more subtle aspects of form—irony and detail depicting human faces, gestures, and figures. It is to lavish words upon clothing, houses, landscapes—any nonhuman objects—in order to associate them with the characters in the novel. And in so far as the Victorian novelist *was* concerned with form and method, he regarded them only as craft. But to Virginia Woolf, her "new method and form" was a new morality, and asking her to invest her characters "with Victorian thoroughness" is unreasonable.

Since "craft" and "morality" were synonymous in Bloomsbury's liturgy, the equation, though not as revolutionary as Bloomsbury believed, was authentically non-Victorian. A fictional character, George Eliot's Adam Bede, appearing in 1859, made the equation his credo.

Adam, however, an intelligent but rustic carpenter, was neither blessed nor afflicted with heightened consciousness and was especially innocent of the intricacies and problems attending the creation of novels. But when the form of a novel is regarded as moral, the parallel with Adam's doctrine of ethical work disappears. Morality is creed, method, discipline, and purpose. When boards are sawed, planed, and joined into an honestly and well-made cabinet, an action which can even be regarded as "thorough," the product can be regarded as moral. But the metaphorical sawing, planing, and joining in the writing of Virginia Woolf's early novels is a small part of her craft and has nothing at all to do with her sensibility, another element that enters into the equation of aesthetic practice and morality. As for the finished "product," her novels, they are not comparable to a well-made cabinet. They are as fragile and continuously changing, as they are read, as life itself. Even if, in the ordinary sense, their forms be fixed and stable, the definition and perception of them vary with the historical and personal viewpoint of the reader. Perhaps in the future heightened or expanded literary understanding will reconcile in the novel "Victorian thoroughness" with method and form elevated to morality, but neither Virginia Woolf, Forster's essay on her early work, nor *Aspects of the Novel* has shown the way.

Moreover, Forster's oblique reservations about Virginia Woolf's early novels can be viewed as a dialectic between Forster the novelist and Forster the critic. A continuation of the process is implicit in "Ibsen the Romantic" (1928). Forster observes, "If a writer has a romantic temperament, he will find human relationships beautiful. His characters may hate one another . . . but will generate nobility . . . they will never be squalid. . . . And the crux in Ibsen is that, though he had the romantic temperament, he found personal intercourse sordid" (*AH, p. 100*).

Although Leonard Bast lives in squalor, he never becomes sordid. He is finally liberated from even the danger of sordidness because Forster's temperament is either romantic or sympathetic to the attribute in other people. In his own way, Leonard aspires to "human relations," which to Forster have always signified the opposite of sordidness. And indeed, the attitudes of the other characters in *Howards End* finally "generate nobility" in Leonard.

With his experience as novelist as background, Forster's critique of Ibsen can more readily be discussed. Just as Forster wove together his own attitudes and technique to create Leonard—to make his point about Ibsen—Forster subtly transposes the man and his work. He notes Ibsen's romantic temperament, and in conclusion focuses on the work by talking about the man. Forster's critical method may startle or annoy some readers, but it is eminently characteristic of him.

In "T. S. Eliot" (1928) the center of the discussion is not Eliot's poetry and prose but Huysman's *A Rebours*. When he was a Red Cross volunteer in Egypt during World War I, Forster sprained his ankle and was cosseted for three weeks in the charming garden of a friend. Forster's description of the episode is wry, but his recollection of reading *A Rebours* during his recuperation is emotional and creates one of the autobiographical glimpses that divide people who respond sympathetically to Forster from those who do not.

Forster was not Hemingway at Caporetto, and a sprained ankle followed by temporary withdrawal from even secondhand experience of the War does not suggest heroism, which Forster in any case does not claim. But the man of sensibility experiences attrition and strain even at the fringe of a war, just as the physically engaged fighting man, dogged or courageous, does.

About reading *A Rebours*, Forster writes, "The waves of edifying bilge rolled off me, the newspapers ebbed . . . and something resembling reality took their place. Perhaps it was not real, but it was not helpful, and in 1917 that was enough to make me repeat after the muezzin on my minaret 'Thank God' " (*AH, p.* 106).

Forster's report of *A Rebours* is not an accurate critique. Des Esseintes does on occasion exercise will, and with savage purpose. He is unable to function in society, but he hates it (Huysmans began as Zola's disciple). Only des Esseintes' experiments with his feelings in the privacy of his house faintly resemble Forster's seclusion in his Cairo garden and illuminate Forster's assertion that des Esseintes "ignored the will" and "had time to experiment with his feelings" (*AH, p. 106*).

But it is, however, understandable that Forster, reminiscing, should emphasize the latter aspect of *A Rebours*. His hatred of propaganda, of the sights, sounds, and smells of war reaching him, had required, for him to go on, a continuous effort of the will. Recalling his garden, he is as much selective as inaccurate when he neglects the fact that des Esseintes' animosity toward society is an exercise of will.

Is it too speculative to see also a link between the ignored will and the characters in Forster's novels? Philip Herriton and Rickie ignore the will. Lucy Honeychurch does not, but when her will leads to a wrong course of action and is revealed to be in actuality the will of others, she changes direction.

As for time to be oneself, men at war discover that time is fevered, empty, foreshortened, measured by a single day. In Forster's characterization of Stephen Wonham, if not in the discussion of "story" in *Aspects of the Novel*, an individual sense of time is essential to personality. The soldier, even the Red Cross worker in Cairo, is deprived of the freedom to experience time in accordance with the needs of his own nature.

More important, however, is that during the remainder of the War and the years that have followed Forster has not imitated des Esseintes' retreat. Forster's withdrawal—if it can be called that—has been a quest, in reflective repose, for personal and political truth. And his seclusion has hardly been complete. He has appeared at the lecture stand of international conferences, responded to requests for radio broadcasts, signed his name to petitions for causes he has believed in, and welcomed with warm hospitality a variety of visitors.

As literary critic, he has been flexible and alert to changing events. To say this is to praise him. Since World War I, these events have succeeded each other with a rapidity reducing to silence younger and more allegedly active men of letters. However, except on a few occasions, when he has risen to a particular challenge, he has become less interested in critical theory. He has become more inclined to indulge his proclivity for eclecticism and his humanistic interest in whatever aspect of fiction seems most appropriate to discuss at a given moment. Perceiving in 1934 the oncoming threat to Western culture, he wrote, "The propping quality in books . . . is . . . a by-product of . . . their power to give pleasure. . . . Art is not enough, any more than love is enough, and thought isn't stronger than artillery parks. . . . But art, . . . the most nervous of the three . . . is not all gossamer. . . . it has become part of our armour, and we can gird it on, although there is no armour against Fate" (AH, p. 89).

Such statements have provoked debate about whether or not Forster is an effective twentieth-century voice. Those who insist that art should aggressively combat barbarism censure Forster's skepticism. Skepticism, however, is not equatable with pessimism. It is, rather, an attempt to define the truth and the positive value of art. To some critics Forster's description of art as "armour" signifies passive defeatism. But others will see in his phrase "the propping quality of books" an assertion that art enables the self to retain its integrity when confronted by "artillery parks." Activity also reflects a man's position, and it is fair to note that many writers in the '30's were more vigorously engaged in combatting barbarism—some simply because they were younger—then was Forster. But the last word should be that his contribution and theirs ought not to be weighed on the same scale. Furthermore, if the difference could be measured, it would be shadowed in any retrospective view. Forster's unassuming eloquence helped establish for the life and renewal of culture a much higher priority among human concerns, in the years just following 1934, than culture might otherwise have been given.

In *Abinger Harvest*, the last collected entry is *The Abinger Pageant* (1934), a pageant play. With it, Forster returns home. He does so out of love of place and English tradition and out of his ingrained domesticity (his home at the time was the Surrey village of Abinger Hammer).

Abinger Pageant reveals once more Forster's partiality to tableaux. The play is a static sequence of six scenes, framed by a prologue and an epilogue, and it tells the history of England through the centuries by focusing on one village. But the play indicates that when Forster creates a tableau, it should be subordinated within the format of a novel. The tableaux in his novels are few and are dramatic moments, turning points in plot, and sources of energy moving the narrative forward. Strung together in *The Abinger Pageant*, they simply constitute an unsuccessful, if slight and unassuming, drama. However, this suggests another consideration—Forster as dramatist—and it should be noted that his novels have been dramatized with surprising success,[9] although the work has been done by other hands or in collaboration.[10] Equally relevant, to Forster as dramatist, are the distinguished librettos he has written.[11]

One thread of continuity in *The Abinger Pageant* is trees, a persistent theme and inspiration to his imagination in a great part of his work. For example, in "Other Kingdom" Evelyn escapes Harcourt Worters by turning into a tree. In "The Road from Colonus," the hollow tree is the central object. Rickie Elliot tells Agnes that he has written a story about a dryad. The wych-elm that protects Howards End has the distinction of being one of the few symbols in Forster's work that he has acknowledged as such. When Mrs. Moore leaves Bombay, coconut palms wave good-by and tell her that they have nothing in common with the Marabar Caves. Marianne Thornton feared as a child that if Napoleon invaded England he would cut down the tulip tree at Battersea Rise.

Although replete with thematic and Freudian interest, trees do not relate to Forster as a literary critic. His pageant plays, despite their creative form, do. In 1940 he wrote a second, *England's Green and Pleasant Land*. Like the first, its chief purpose is to "protest against the destruction of the land and the old landmarks and ways of life by 'progress.'" [12] Forster's writing for this reason is analagous to his critical impulse to protest or praise, with its end in view, the process forming a work of literature.

More explicitly relevant to Forster as literary judge is his return, in a 1947 lecture titled "The *Raison D'Etre* of Criticism in the Arts," [13] to questions of theory unevenly treated twenty years earlier in *Aspects of the Novel*. But the lecture is weakened internally by random associations. "One must allow [criticism] to construct aesthetic theories" (*TC, p. 108*), Forster asserts, but warns against the danger to creative writers of such theories. He concludes with a coda to his lifelong approach to literary theory, "The construction of aesthetic theories and their comparison are desirable cultural excersises: the theories themselves are unlikely to . . . hinder or help" (*TC, p. 109*).

If it is only a pleasurable vocation, why be serious about criticism? Aware of the question, Forster offers an alternative to his first view. "A more practical activity for criticism is the sensitive dissection of particular works of art" (*TC, p. 109*). But Forster disclaims his own ability to carry on this activity. His honesty, though engaging, is disappointing. He has not confronted the question we would most like to hear him discuss, how the humanist relates man and literature. When Forster proceeds to distinguish the creative artist from the critic, our hopes rise. Here is a possible approach to the question. Both artists and critics are human beings related to the nonhuman work of art. But Forster disappoints us again. He simply discusses the subconscious element in creative work and repeats that the critic can be of no important help to the artist.

Aware perhaps that he had failed in his final attempt to relate human individuals and individual works of art, in 1949 he adopted the only sensible and viable position for himself. He substituted "society" for the personality that in reality experiences art. He changed the problem.

A person in daily life and a "person" in art are both

concrete entities. Society, however, is an abstraction, and no special intellectual power is needed to contrast the concrete with the abstract. But when Forster contrasts them, his style and tone transform the commonplace, "I believe in art for art's sake" (*TC, p. 88*), but this does not mean that only art matters. He names the difference between art and politically structured society, "Order . . . is something evolved from within . . . and in the social and political category it has never existed except for the convenience of historians" . . . (*TC, p. 90*). Works of art are the only objects in the material universe to possess internal order.

Despite the farewell, implicit in the stress on society, to the problem of relating an actual person to a fictional one, an apologia for Forster is in order. What is lost if art claims autonomy and the man in daily life goes about his business, oblivious that he has not been philosophically connected with a man in fiction resembling him? Although many insistent minds, like Spinoza's, Kant's, and Coleridge's, have been unwilling to regard the world as an aggregate of discontinuous entities, no theory interrelating these entities has yet endured. The cosmic vision evades us, and if Forster has been unsuccessful with a small corner of it—the connection between people in daily life and in art—other critics and theorists have fared no better. Forster at least has told us not to deprive ourselves of pleasure in art while we accept social responsibilities and await the visionary who will relate for us all things.

Thus, during the past half century of strident, puritanical, and religiously fanatic clashes over the subject of how man in daily life relates to characters in fiction, Forster has offered repose and balance. As a literary critic, he has been dismissed, often contemptuously. But if the fragmentation and chaos of values, the blinding scorn and distorting anger of our own day are ever revealed as historical steps toward something constructive—communication or nonrepressive order—Forster will be remembered as an important "presence" among literary critics contemporary with him. And in retrospect, his stature will increase.

Despite his credentials—he read history at Cambridge—Forster has probably exasperated as many professional historians as literary critics. The problem is not that people rather than institutions or forces dominate his historical essays. Many an accredited historian has used the same technique. The problem is that Forster charmingly invades the minds and hearts of historical persons. He mantles the past with the present and vice versa. He expertly introduces fact, only to vaporize it into Forsterian tones and values.

By 1920 he had formulated an inimitable view of history. "It is pleasant to be transferred from an office where one is afraid of the sergeant-major into an office where one can intimidate generals, and perhaps this is why History is so attractive to the more timid amongst us. We can recover self-confidence by snubbing the dead. The captains and the kings depart at our slightest censure, while as for the 'hosts of minor officials' . . . we heed them not, although in actual life they entirely block our social horizon" (AH, p. 191).

This is historiography grounded in the Freudian confessional and in British manners. Through whimsy and fantasy Forster depicts history as a contest between himself, powerful men, and the faceless men around them. He is not detached. Although Forster would snub the dead (not really in fact), he brings them back to life, actually to manage them. Their revival, however, can be sustained only by infusing them with Forster's own life. Moreover, Forster enters into personal relations with his resurrected figures.

In disrepute during the '30's and '40's, a method of writing history roughly similar to Forster's but more astringent has been revived today. It is doubtful, however, that any contemporary historian so liberally introduces into the process so many intimate sides of himself as does Forster. And none, it is certain, writes in Forster's tone— one of the authentically individual and distinguishing aspects of all his work.

In his relations with historical persons, objects are often touchstones for the Forsterian aura. And his own interests become rhetorical questions that should be answered by the dead but are answered wryly or with acute practical psychology by Forster.

In "Macolnia Stops" (1903), an Etruscan toilet case evokes for him the spirit of Pan, important in Forster's short stories and in *The Longest Journey* (at one point Stephen is touched by Pan); and emphasized during the late nineteenth- and early twentieth-century revival of Hellenism that affected Cambridge.[14] The relic evokes also friendship, Forster's cherished discovery at Cambridge. But through these associations, a matron and her daughter come to life. Recreating their minds and feelings, while expressing his own interests, Forster achieves the slight but essential shift of viewpoint that places his subjects in antiquity and distinguishes them from himself, "Dindia Macolnia and her daughter, if Etruscan antiquities reflect truly, agreed with the little Pan. They did not understand water, and it is not likely that they understood Friendship either, which is the second motive that their toilet case reveals to us to-day" (*AH, p. 197*).

Forster's recreation of historical persons by focusing on an object is a prose counterpart to Keats's method in "Ode on a Grecian Urn." In addition, had Forster not indulged poetic license quite as largely and freely as he did, he might be included in the school of R. G. Collingwood. But what ought to be noted finally is the mark of all Forster's historical writing; it is intimately sympathetic and tolerant.

Sympathy and tolerance, however, have a psychological underside, a feeling that those toward whom we direct them have not achieved as high a degree of sensibility, perception, or awareness as we have. Thus, when Forster evokes the dead, even those remarkable for their original-ity, he seldom permits them self-understanding equal to his comprehension of them. He does not snub the dead. He merely makes certain that through a consciousness larger than theirs he will control them and that his per-sonal relations with them will never result in a debate lost by him.

Another way of putting the matter is to say that Forster's tolerance and sympathy do not exclude judgment. But it is the kind that in novels discloses the mood and tone of the author. In "Gemistus Pletho" (1905), Forster not only applies this kind of judgment but in the process of elaborating it approaches the poetic prose of his novels. He gives as much information as might be expected from a professional historian. Nonetheless, writing of Gemistus Pletho, who tried to incorporate Greek myth into Christianity, Forster envelopes with transparent clouds a story of intrigue, travel, conferences, and accommodations to each other among powerful people. Through the clouds, the light of Forster's Cambridge shines and competes with Gemistus Pletho as much as it illuminates him, "Gemistus tried to recall antiquity by . . . the names of the Greek gods. . . . If he is absurd, it is in a touching way; his dream of antiquity is grotesque and incongruous, but it has a dream's intensity, and something of a dream's imperishable value" (AH, p. 218).

Not only Forster's tone but Gemistus Pletho's career resemble the characterization of Rickie Elliot. Both Gemistus and Rickie, according to Forster, were divided men who were ineffective in life and reached no apotheosis in death that could erase their past errors. But each left a legacy—his writing—and created loyal remembrance of themselves. Rickie won Stephen's heart. Gemistus died in 1450 in New Sparta (Mistrà). A Renaissance heretic, Sismondo Malatesta, whose spiritual radicalism anticipated Stephen's, "captured Mistrà . . . and, out of [his] great love . . . for Gemistus, exhumed his body and translated it to Italy" (AH, p. 218).

To Forster, Renaissance Italy is the human achievement worthy of the awe and respect he accords to the earth—and to those, like Stephen, who are close to the earth. In a sense, too, Stephen, by publishing Rickie's stories about getting close to nature reconciles Rickie with the earth and thus posthumously "saves" him. Gemistus had lived in the "medieval world [surveying] the empty site of Sparta," and was buried amidst the new Renaissance splendor, "behind the marble arcades of Alberti" (*AH, p. 218*). The resemblance between Forster's historical and fictional Hellenists tempts a reconsideration of Forster's distinction, in *Aspects*, between the "historical" side of a person and the hidden side of him exposed by novelists.

However, in other essays, moralism counters poetry in Forster as historian. In 1905 he wrote about Girolamo Cardan, a harried and afflicted man. To underscore Cardan's high morality in truly essential matters and to establish Cardan as a victim, Forster describes Cardan's moral failings. Forster's seemingly paradoxical method is based on confidence rather than quixoticism.

Amidst a detailed account of Cardan's unattractive traits, Forster tells us that "Cardan had the head to know that it was wrong, and the heart to be sorry for it" (*AH, p. 223*). In this respect Cardan is unlike Herbert Pembroke; the complex character of the Renaissance Italian is not caused by the primal curse of good-and-evil. Illegitimate, he "was the victim of snobbishness, which, if it is not coeval with human nature, may be dated from the Counter-Reformation" (*AH, p. 225*).

Forster's ironic reference to the Counter Reformation is not only playfulness but technique. It counteracts the sprawling time-span "snobbishness . . . coeval with human nature." It refocuses our attention on the historical moment and place of Cardan's life. It suggestively evolves twentieth-century England out of the Counter Reformation. Wisely, however, Forster leaves the suggestion allusive, introduces it as a tonal variation as he creates the cultural and historical context for Cardan's portrait. To develop the suggestion would take more space than Forster is willing to give and would require a temperament different from his. And even if undertaken by an earnest and literal-minded historian, the development might decline into irrelevant and unconvincing speculations.

Besides poetry and morality, "place" is a central interest for Forster, a fact noted in connection with his other writing. His love of "place" contributes to *Alexandria*

(1922). But it is divided into a "guide" and a "history," and although the first section does emphasize locations, buildings, and monuments, the second reflects other characteristics of Forster's historical writing. The "history" [15] is an evocation of individuals who lived in Alexandria or influenced it. Not surprisingly, the best of the portraits depend on the personal relations of the subjects and, like Forster in his role as historian, these individuals conduct their relations with intelligence and sensibility superior to their intimates'.[16] The people portrayed not only win Forster's admiration, they almost equal him.

Admiration, however, is not respect. The latter, in Forster's historical writing, is associated only with "domesticity," a fact which creates a true paradox. For Forster, domesticity begins in the nineteenth century and with figures in his own family background or with people associated with his forebears. Since neither group compares in historical importance with the persons of earlier times he has created, the paradox is that he reserves respect for relatively minor figures. A touch of apology or defensiveness therefore marks his writing about the English nineteenth century, his family, and their associates.

Like his biography of Marianne Thornton, "Mrs. Hannah More" (1928) illustrates the almost reflexive respect with which Forster responds to domesticity. Godmother of Marianne Thornton, member of the Clapham sect, Mrs. More in "her work . . . was good. . . . She taught the poor to read and wash . . . and before her day no one had taught them anything. . . . Her desire to meddle in their affairs was mixed with genuine pity and affection, and in some ways she came nearer to them than do those who approach them with respect . . ." (AH, p. 276).

By analogy, the last clause is revealing. It suggests that the paradox inherent in his respectful treatment of figures like Mrs. More associated with his feeling for domesticity is really a disinclination to get as close to them as he did to Macolnia, Gemistus Pletho, and Cardan, whose privacy he willingly trespassed through poetic license. The closer Forster gets to home, the less inclined he becomes to

suggest that his own consciousness is superior to his subject's and is in control. As historian, he never did intimidate or snub captains and kings, but he transferred back to
the sergeant-major's office (his domestic portraits generally belong to a relatively late period in his career). Not
fearful in this office, but lulled by the confining routine of
the familiar, he substituted loyalty for boldness and inventiveness.

To turn to Forster as social observer is to be exposed
again to the freshness of his early comments and to witness him developing along a path different from the one
he followed as historian. Despite his frequent references to
political issues, he has remained detached from parties
and doctrinaire positions. One explanation offered for the
fact is that his outlook has been founded on a "broad ideal
of individualism, not . . . class snobbery." [17] As social
critic, he has been as liberated and inventive as he has
been as a writer of fiction.

In "Notes on the English Character" (1920), Forster
asks if the English are hypocritical. He answers the question, paradoxically for the sake of truth, by using political
strategy. He examines the query, decides it is superficial,
and reformulates it: "Do we mean *conscious* deceit? . . .
The English are comparatively guiltless of this. . . . Do
we mean *unconscious* deceit? Muddle-headedness? Of this
I believe them to be guilty" (*AH, p. 20*).

"Muddle-headedness," a continuous theme in Forster's
work, is here a social concept. But it is not a judgment, as
a conventional or superficial verdict that the English are
hypocritical would have been. As social observer, Forster
attempts to understand what is, and only incidentally to
suggest what ought to be.

Although "My Wood" (1926) is autobiographical, it is
also a comment on social actuality. Forster has purchased
some land. He feels heavy but wants to increase his hold-
ings. Is this a contradiction? Hardly, for he is examining
his all too human desires and relating them to materialism, a perennially central social idea always requiring reconsideration but rigidified in the '20's into a platitude,

"Creation, property, enjoyment form a sinister trinity. . . . Creation and enjoyment . . . are [however] often unattainable without a material basis . . . [which] is forced on us . . . by the feeling that in property may lie the germs of self-development. . . . Our life . . . is, and ought to be, material and carnal. But . . . our materialism and carnality . . . are still entangled with the desire for ownership, where (in the words of Dante) 'Possession is one with loss' " (AH, pp. 35–36).

By discussing character and society, Forster has made materialism meaningful and has reminded us that men experience the spiritual through matter. But he has said also that society (although he has asserted elsewhere it harbors no internal order) ought to have a consistent and intelligent approach to problems of the human personality. It does not, and only Dante's religious dogma, true but beyond man's capability to translate into practice, explains why, just as the synthesis of myth and reality explains the inadequacies of the middle class in *Howards End* but does not offer a concrete and visible solution. "My Wood" might have been written by Margaret and a Henry Wilcox she has radically transformed. The suggestion is not gratuitous. *Howards End* is the novel by Forster that asks questions about property.

But as "The Second Darkness" approached, Forster substituted existential questions for metaphysical ones. "One must behave as if one is immortal," he wrote in "Liberty in England" (1935), "and as if civilization is eternal. Both statements are false . . . both . . . must be assumed . . . true if we are to . . . keep open a few breathing holes for the human spirit" (AH, p. 85).

His quasi-existentialism should not, however, lead to a careless belief that he ever accepted or developed the idea of the absurd—any more than Camus, whose humanism was more complex, came at the end of his life to rest upon the concept. But the comparison is a limited one. In 1935, at the extreme verge of humane skepticism, Forster remained rooted in his lifelong experience and did not explore, as he often did at other times, the subtle historical changes implicit in the approach of "The Second Darkness." Camus, as his essential humanism became more evident, remained sensitive and responsive, even to an excessive degree, to every slight shift in the winds touching his consistently interrelated personal problems and social consciousness.

Forster's recurrence to the self created by "the fag-end of Victorian liberalism" [18] — even his 1935 existentialism had already been expressed by Mr. Emerson in 1908 and can be found also in Meredith's poetry[19] — may explain Forster's brief eclipse in the late '30's. But nothing will readily explain his restoration as a social critic during World War II, although John Beer has at least provided a possible clue. "His broadcasts . . . struck a new note in wartime apologetic. . . . where heroics counted for less than ever before . . . his type of unassuming firmness had a symbolic value." [20]

In these broadcasts, Forster is neither strident nor exhortatory. Candid appraisals of England and Germany go side by side. When appropriate, humor lightens his talks. Casually refusing to force the truth to expose itself, he effectively reveals the difference between Western culture and Nazism. As a result, while the well-intentioned words of many a professional wartime propagandist are now in oblivion, Forster's broadcasts are still read.

But with respect to Forster's reemergence as social commentator during World War II, perception of the qualities of his broadcasts come to us through hindsight. Perhaps the explanation for his reachieving stature in World War II is that Forster as artist, not social critic, was rediscovered, and that in retrospect the distinction between his two roles has been blurred. Nostalgic for the literary excitement of the '20's, knowing Forster best through *Passage,* the generation that fought World War II did at the time acclaim Forster a "modern." These readers incongruously associated him with Eliot, Pound, and Joyce; and, more plausibly, with D. H. Lawrence and Virginia Woolf. It would seem that the renewal of Forster's reputation during the War was caused by ignorance

or by some process of cultural history we do not understand. As both social critic and novelist, Forster today is
often called a late Victorian. Although the term "Victorian" has recently lost its sting, it was opprobious twenty-
five years ago, and few would have thought then of apply-
ing it to Forster.

In his postwar position he has not radically changed,
but the luck, fumbling, or mystery favoring him during
the middle '40's has carried over and supplied him with a
continuous audience. As a literary critic, he has continued
to prevail, in a milieu of petty fragmentation, by providing
the balance of his presence—a fact previously noted. In all
areas, he continues to explain what he perceives, experiences, or avoids. He unassumingly persists in declining to
judge England's and the world's ills or to offer practical
remedies. But we, in contrast, must judge Forster as a
social critic. And however grateful posterity may be to
Forster for unmasking social clichés and describing accurately and in depth "what is," a social critic, during his
own lifetime, is obliged to be sharp and active.

Forster knows that he lacks activism and the intellectual zest for the processes of political intrigue that combine with reflection in the best and even most high-
minded social critics. Self-knowledge has intensified in
him an intermittent melancholy that an agressive man
would experience less frequently or not at all in our
progressively more wretched twentieth century. Forster's
dejection is evident in one of the undated notes at the
conclusion to *Two Cheers*, "I waddle on under a ruck-sack
of traditional nature-emotions, and try to find something
important in the English countryside—man-made, easily
alterable by man. George Meredith, my predecessor on
these downs, could upset himself with a better conscience" (*TC, p. 358*).

But whatever light this confession of temporary depression may cast on Forster as social critic, let it be said by
way of restoring balance to our judgment of his performance in the role that it would be captious to make too
much of his passive melancholy. The sensitive, the wise,

and even the fools not yet insensible agree in deploring what man has done to the English countryside. Only knaves are complacent and satisfied.

Let us not harp on Forster's insufficiencies as a social critic. To overemphasize the arbitrary division of his roles is to obscure the subtle effectiveness of his entire career, including the years after he stopped publishing novels. During his lifetime, he has successfully outfaced many challenges to humanism. He has been one of the saving remnant who have kept it alive. In conclusion to an essay on Forster, F. R. Leavis, not known in general as Forster's advocate, has said that the humane tradition "really is, for all its weakness, the indispensable transmitter of something that humanity cannot afford to lose." [21]

Paraphrasing Leavis, the question is, which authors can we not afford to lose? Perhaps abstractly the query is an idle one, because we are not aware of those we have not read or who have for some reason failed to affect our cultural ambience. We can recognize the sadness of speculative loss only when we think of writers whose works we know intimately. However, the question is not idle when asked about Forster. He has affected the twentieth century and has been read and reread by members of two or three generations—depending on how one defines a generation—who would readily assert they could not afford to lose him.

Nevertheless, the abstract view is relevant. As is the case with any other author, we are ignorant of who or what we would have been without Forster. His weaknesses and failures cannot be overlooked. He does not appeal to some of our most distinguished critics. Whether or not he is part of the sensibility of those who dislike his work is difficult to say; the answer perhaps depends on the individual and cannot be discovered among generic attitudes. But for those who have been troubled by the assault upon humanism in the twentieth century, Forster has helped make it historically more sophisticated. To this extent he is, for many readers, an author they would have been the worse for not knowing.

Despite its sophistication, however, his humanism is not easily adopted—by anyone. Always weakened to a degree by his almost infinite tolerance and by his casualness about theoretical matters, his humanism today is less able to cope with the contemporary savagery in art and society.

Only if a day of greater purpose and coherence in art and society ever arrives will Forster's achievement, through the traditional process of comparison, be properly assessable. During the last fifty odd years, his accomplishment *has* been assessed—and reassessed. But common sense, tolerance for radical experiments in art and society, whatever value we individually find in them, and uncertainty about the world revolution in all values now going on advise a temporary halt in large reevaluations of Forster's life and work.

If the world survives and the historical development of humanism resumes—tomorrow or in a future generation—revaluations of Forster's life and work will again be appropriate. But this will mean that Forster's own faith in mankind, as well as his art, has been vindicated. It is a possibility devoutly to be desired.

1—Introductions

1. E. M. Forster, "The Second Darkness," *Two Cheers for Democracy* (New York, 1951), p. 56.

2. E. H. Johnson, "The Intelligent Mr. E. M. Forster," *Personalist*, xxxv (January 1954), 51.

3. Lionel Trilling, *E. M. Forster* (London, 1944), p. 21.

4. V. S. Pritchett, "Mr. Forster's New Year," *New Statesman and Nation*, LVI (December 27, 1958), 912.

5. J. B. Beer, *The Achievement of E. M. Forster* (London, 1962), pp. 14–15.

6. F. C. Crews, *E. M. Forster: The Perils of Humanism* (Princeton, 1962), p. 8.

7. E. M. Forster, *Marianne Thornton: A Domestic Biography: 1797–1887* (New York, 1956), p. vii. Subsequent page references are to this edition.

8. Molly Painter-Downes, "Profiles: Kingsman," *The New Yorker*, xxxv (September 19, 1959), 52.

9. Since the manuscript of the present study was completed, Wilfred Stone's excellent book on Forster has been published. (*The Cave and the Mountain* (Stanford, 1966.) I have not tried to make full use of this work but have indicated in these notes references to Stone's book that seem particularly valuable. For the reference here, Chapter II of *The Cave and the Mountain* (pp. 21–39) is particularly of interest.

10. E. M. Forster, *Goldsworthy Lowes Dickenson* (London, 1962), p. 25.

11. *Ibid.*, p. 26.

12. *Ibid.*, p. 35.

13. Beer, *The Achievement of E. M. Forster*, p. 20.

14. H. J. Oliver, *The Art of E. M. Forster* (Melbourne, 1960), pp. 3–4.

15. J. K. Johnstone, *The Bloomsbury Group: A Study of E. M. Forster, Lytton Strachey, Virginia Woolf, and their Circle* (New York, 1954), p. 42.

16. Trilling, *E. M. Forster* (London, 1944), p. 12.

17. See also Stone, *The Cave and the Mountain*, pp. 63–65.

18. Johnstone, *The Bloomsbury Group*, p. 30.

19. Beer, *The Achievement of E. M. Forster*, p. 172.

20. *Ibid.*, p. 205.

21. In addition to interviews cited in the text, see also Stone, pp. 41 n, 52 n, 55 n.

22. K. W. Gransden, "E. M. Forster at Eighty," *Encounter*, XII (January 1959), 77.

23. David Jones, "E. M. Forster on his Life and his Books," *The Listener*, LXI (January 1, 1959), 11.

24. *Ibid.*, p. 11.

25. See also Painter-Downes, "Profiles: Kingsman," 72. He "constantly goes back to his favorite Austen."

26. Jones, "E. M. Forster on his Life and his Books," 11.

27. Angus Wilson, "A Conversation with E. M. Forster," *Encounter*, IX (November 1957), 55.

28. *Ibid.*, p. 56.

29. All the information recorded here is taken from an interview with Forster, printed in *Writers at Work: The Paris Review Interviews* (New York, 1959), pp. 23–35. This quotation is from p. 23.

30. In addition, Stone says that a "completed but unpublished novel dealing with the subject of homosexuality was produced after *Passage*, and at least one unpublished short story." *The Cave and the Mountain*, p. 347 n.

31. Furbank and Haskell, *Writers at Work*, p. 34.

32. *Ibid.*, p. 35.

33. John Fuller, "E. M. Forster at Seventy," *Adelphi*, XXVIII (May 1952), 593.

34. Jones, "E. M. Forster on his Life and his Books," 12.

35. Pritchett, "Mr. Forster's New Year," 913.

2—Short Stories and Arctic Summer

1. E. M. Forster, *Collected Short Stories* (London, 1954), p. 5. All subsequent page references to the short stories are to this edition.

2. Alan Wilde, *Art and Order: A Study of E. M. Forster* (New York, 1964), p. 7.

3. See Wilfred E. Stone, *The Cave and the Mountain* (Stanford, 1966) p. 53 on *The Independent Review* and Forster.

4. E. M. Forster, *Goldsworthy Lowes Dickenson* (London, 1962), pp. 115–16.

5. See references to "new dawn" in discussion of *Arctic Summer*, p. 59 of this chapter.

6. Lionel Trilling, *E. M. Forster* (London, 1944), p. 35.

7. The date and place of the first publication of Forster's stories have been presented in a concise and thorough form in Alan Wilde's *Art and Order*, p. 62n. For the convenience of the reader, Wilde's listing, as well as his notes, are given here.

> According to Forster, the stories were all written before the First World War. The dates of their publication are as follows (* indicates that the story appeared in *The Celestial Omnibus,* ** that it appeared in *The Eternal Moment*):
>
> 1903 "Albergo Empedocle," *Temple Bar*
> 1904 "The Story of a Panic," *The Independent Review**
>   "The Road from Colonus," *The Independent Review**
>   "The Other Side of the Hedge," *The Independent Review**
> 1905 "The Eternal Moment," *The Independent Review***
> 1907 "The Curate's Friend," *Putnam's Magazine**
> 1908 "The Celestial Omnibus," *The Albany Review**
> 1909 "Other Kingdom," *The English Review**
>   "The Machine Stops," *The Oxford and Cambridge Review***
> 1911 "The Point of It," *The English Review***
>   "Mr. Andrews," *The Open Window***
> 1912 "Cooperation," *The English Review***
> 1920 "The Story of the Siren," *The Hogarth Press***

Wilde also says the name of "Cooperation" was later changed to "Co-ordination." "The Story of a Panic" was, according to Forster, the first written of his tales. K. W. Gransden in his *E. M. Forster* (1962) p. 11, refers to an unpublished story, "The Rock."

To the above information should be added the following facts. *The Celestial Omnibus,* Forster's first collection of stories, was published in 1911; his second, *The Eternal Moment,* in 1928.

8. Trilling, *E. M. Forster*, p. 37.

9. E. M. Forster, "Albergo Empedocle," *Temple Bar*, cxxviii (December, 1903), 664.

10. *Ibid.*, pp. 670–71.   11. *Ibid.*, p. 678.

12. "Arctic Summer," Fragment of an Unfinished Novel, *Tribute to Benjamin Britten on His Fiftieth Birthday* (London, 1963), p. 55.

13. *Ibid.*, p. 54.   14. *Ibid.*, p. 54.   15. *Ibid.*, p. 50.

16. *Ibid.*, p. 53.

17. *Ibid.*, p. 53.

18. See Stone, *The Cave and the Mountain*, p. 53. ". . . Bloomsbury liberalism was emphatically a liberalism of ideas detached from political engagement."

3 – Where Angels Fear to Tread

1. It would be well, at this point, to clarify, as much as possible, the relationship between the order of publication of his first three novels to the order in which Forster worked upon them. K. W. Gransden has accurately summarized the pertinent information. "Forster's two Italian novels, *Where Angels Fear to Tread* (1905) and *A Room with a View* (1908), are, in order of publication, his first and third novels; we know, however, that he drafted the Italian part of *A Room with a View* in 1903" but put it aside till he had published *The Longest Journey* in 1907. *E. M. Forster* (New York, 1962), p. 22.

2. Lionel Trilling, *E. M. Forster* (London, 1944), p. 51.

3. *Ibid.*, p. 58.

4. Gransden, *E. M. Forster* (New York, 1962), p. 26.

5. E. M. Forster, *Where Angels Fear to Tread* (London, 1947), p. 74. All subsequent page references to the novel are to this edition.

6. Trilling, *E. M. Forster*, p. 55.

7. J. B. Beer, *The Achievement of E. M. Forster* (London, 1962), p. 74.

8. See E. M. Forster, *Aspects of the Novel* (London, 1953), p. 155.

9. Trilling, *E. M. Forster*, p. 66.

10. Harry T. Moore, *E. M. Forster* (New York, 1965), p. 21.

11. Trilling, *E. M. Forster*, p. 52.

4—The Longest Journey

1. E. M. Forster, "Introduction," *The Longest Journey* (London, 1960), p. ix.

2. *Ibid.*, pp. ix–x.

3. E. M. Forster, *The Longest Journey* (London, 1947) p. 7. Subsequent page references to the novel are to this edition.

4. Lionel Trilling, *E. M. Forster* (London, 1944), p. 68.

5. See Wilfred Stone, *The Cave and the Mountain* (Stanford, 1966) pp. 65–66 on Moore's actual influence upon Forster.

6. "Introduction," *The Longest Journey*, p. xi.

7. See Stone's conversations with Forster about his school. (*The Cave and the Mountain*, p. 43 n).

8. Trilling, *E. M. Forster*, p. 77.

9. *Ibid.*, p. 77.

10. See Stone, *The Cave and the Mountain*, p. 383, for another allusion to the Oedipus problem in Forster's writing—an allusion that associates Forster and D. H. Lawrence.

11. K. W. Gransden, *E. M. Forster* (New York, 1962), p. 48.

12. *Ibid.*, p. 48.

13. P. N. Furbank and F. J. H. Haskell, "E. M. Forster," an interview in *Writers at Work: The Paris Review Interviews*, ed. Malcolm Cowley, (New York, 1959), p. 31.

14. J. B. Beer, *The Achievement of E. M. Forster* (London, 1962), p. 97.

15. Gransden, *E. M. Forster*, p. 50.

5—A Room with a View

1. See E. M. Forster, *Aspects of the Novel* (London, 1949), p. 80.

2. F. C. Crews, *E. M. Forster: The Perils of Humanism* (Princeton, 1962), p. 81.

3. Lee Elbert Holt, "E. M. Forster and Samuel Butler," *PMLA*, LXI (September 1946), 804–19. The words spoken by Mr. Emerson appear on p. 246 of E. M. Forster's *A Room with a View* (London, 1947). All subsequent page references to the novel are to this edition.

4. The resemblances between Meredith's *The Egoist* and *A Room with a View* have often been noted. John Crowe

Ransom, however, has gone further and has discussed in general Forster's relation to Meredith. See Ransom, "E. M. Forster," *Kenyon Review*, v (Autumn 1943), 621–22.

5. Lionel Trilling, *E. M. Forster* (London, 1944), p. 86.

6. Ransom, p. 619.

7. E. M. Forster, "Tourism v. Thuggism," *The Listener*, LVII (January 17, 1957), 124.

8. Trilling, p. 87.

9. K. W. Gransden "E. M. Forster at Eighty," *Encounter*, XII (January 1959), 77.

10. See especially K. W. Gransden, *E. M. Forster* (New York, 1962), p. 33.

11. For further discussion of G. E. Moore, "the good," and Bloomsbury, see especially John Beer, *The Achievement of E. M. Forster* (London, 1962) p. 20; and Wilfred Stone, *The Cave and The Mountain* (Stanford, 1966) pp. 64–65, 109, 120, 230.

6—Howards End

1. E. M. Forster *Howards End* (London, 1947), pp. 47–48. All subsequent page references are to this edition.

2. Lionel Trilling, *E. M. Forster* (London, 1944), p. 102.

3. James Hall, "Forster's Family Reunions," *English Literary History*, xxv (March 1958), p. 63.

4. Trilling, p. 109.

5. Cyrus Hoy, "Forster's Metaphysical Novel," *PMLA*, LXXV (March 1960), 132.

6. See E. K. Brown, *Rhythm in the Novel* (Toronto, 1950), pp. 46–47, 55, 105, 108; and James McConkey, *The Novels of E. M. Forster* (Ithaca, 1957), pp. 117–32 and *passim*.

7. Hoy, p. 130.

8. Frederick McDowell, "The Mild Intellectual Light: Idea and Theme in *Howards End*," *PMLA*, LXXIV (September 1959), 462.

9. *Ibid.*, p. 457.

10. K. W. Gransden, *E. M. Forster* (New York, 1962), pp. 71–72.

11. Harry T. Moore, *E. M. Forster* (New York, 1965), p. 33.

12. Angus Wilson, "The Revolt of Samuel Butler," *The Atlantic Monthly*, CC (November 1957), 198.

13. F. P. McDowell interestingly considers the affinities, in *Howards End*, between Arnold and Forster. See McDowell, "The Mild Intellectual Light," *PMLA* LXXXIV (September 1959), 454, note 7.

14. J. B. Beer, *The Achievement of E. M. Forster*, (London, 162), p. 114.

15. Gransden, *E. M. Forster*, pp. 69–70.

16. See Wilfred Stone, *The Cave and the Mountain* (Stanford, 1966), p. 266.

7—A Passage to India

1. E. M. Forster, *A Passage to India* (New York, 1957), p. xxix.

2. *Ibid.*, p. ix.

3. Lionel Trilling, *E. M. Forster* (London, 1944), p. 138.

4. See, for example, *The Hill of Devi* (New York, 1958) and "Indian Entries," *Encounter*, XVIII (January 1962), pp. 20–27.

5. E. M. Forster, *The Hill of Devi*, p. 238.

6. *A Passage to India* (London, 1947) p. 70. All subsequent page references to the novel are to this edition.

7. *Two Cheers for Democracy* (New York, 1951), p. 68.

8. Quoted by K. Natwar-Singh in an interview with E. M. Forster in *E. M. Forster: A Tribute* (New York, 1964), p. xii.

9. E. M. Forster, *Abinger Harvest* (London, 1953), p. 334.

10. Arnold Kettle, *An Introduction to the English Novel* (London, 1953), II, 153.

11. Nat War-Singh, p. 51.

12. J. B. Priestley, "Review of *A Passage to India*," *The London Mercury*, X (July 1924), 319–20.

13. F. C. Crews, *E. M. Forster: The Perils of Humanism* (Princeton, 1962), p. 153.

14. *Ibid.*, pp. 158–59.

15. Alan Wilde, *Art and Order: A Study of E. M. Forster* (New York, 1964), p. 144.

16. James McConkey, *The Novels of E. M. Forster* (Ithaca, 1957), p. 142.

17. Hugh Maclean, "The Structure of *A Passage to India*," *University of Toronto Quarterly*, XXII (January 1953), 169.

18. McConkey, pp. 153 and 90.

8—Literature, the Past, and the Present

1. V. S. Pritchett, "Mr. Forster's New Year," *New States-man and Nation*, LVI (December 27, 1958), 912.

2. E. M. Forster, *Pharos and Pharillon* 3rd ed. (London, 1961), p. 12.

3. In speaking of the "present"—Forster's—it is worth remembering that he reached maturity at the turn of the century.

4. Forster himself encourages the arrangement of his expository writing under rubrics. The essays he has collected in *Abinger Harvest* (1936) and *Two Cheers for Democracy* (1951) are grouped and subgrouped.

5. E. M. Forster, *Aspects of the Novel* (London, 1949), p. 5. Subsequent page references are to this edition and are incorporated in the text.

6. See introduction to Percy Lubbock's, *The Craft of Fiction* (New York, 1957) for criticism of Forster's concept "aspects of the novel."

7. See especially Wayne C. Booth, *The Rhetoric of Fiction* (Chicago, 1961).

8. E. M. Forster, *Abinger Harvest* (London, 1953), p. 162. Subsequent page references are to this edition and are incorporated in the text.

9. In addition to the successful presentation in England and America of *Passage* as a play, some of Forster's novels have been effectively transformed into dramas for British television.

10. Forster ironically contrasts, in his theatrical transformations, with Meredith and James, both of whom were more ambitious than he to see their work on the stage and neither of whom achieved his remarkable success. There is, no doubt, an aesthetic problem concealed in these facts, but if so, it is a difficult one. Meredith, James, and Forster have been praised equally for their ability to evoke a scene.

11. See P. N. Furbank and F. J. H. Haskell, "E. M. Forster," *Writers at Work: The Paris Review Interviews* (New York, 1959), p. 30 and *Marianne Thornton: A Domestic Biography, 1797–1887* (New York, 1956), p. 301.

12. Wilfred Stone, *The Cave and the Mountain: A Study of E. M. Forster* (Stanford, 1966), p. 365 n.

13. E. M. Forster, *Two Cheers for Democracy* (New York,

1951), p. 107. Subsequent page references are to this edition and are incorporated in the text.

14. See Stone, *The Cave and the Mountain*, p. 134 n on Pan and Hellenism popular around 1903.

15. The book is, incidentally, further evidence of Forster's interest in pageants. He writes, "The 'History' attempts (after the fashion of a pageant) to marshall the activities of Alexandria during the two thousand two hundred and fifty years of her existence." *Alexandria* (New York, 1961), p. xix.

There may be psychological as well as aesthetic basis for Forster's feeling for pageants, and the tableaux associated with them. In *Marianne Thornton*, writing of Christmas tableaux at Battersea Rise, Forster says, "I remember thinking them lovely half a century later, in my own childhood." *Marianne Thornton*, p. 162.

16. One of the best is his characterization of Cleopatra and her relations with Marc Antony. See *Alexandria*, pp. 25–30.

17. F. C. Crews, *E. M. Forster: The Perils of Humanism* (Princeton, 1962), p. 171.

18. E. M. Forster, *Two Cheers for Democracy*, p. 56.

19. For an example of Meredith in an existential mood, see his poem, "The Question Whither."

20. J. B. Beer, *The Achievement of E. M. Forster* (London, 1962), p. 169.

21. F. R. Leavis, "E. M. Forster," *The Common Pursuit* (London, 1962), p. 277.

BIBLIOGRAPHY

<small>WHEN THE</small> first edition of any work quoted or referred to in the text has not been used, the date of original publication is given in parentheses.

WORKS BY E. M. FORSTER

Books

Abinger Harvest. London: Edward Arnold & Co., 1953 (1936).

Alexandria: A History and a Guide. 3rd ed. New York: Doubleday & Co., 1961 (1922).

Aspects of the Novel. London: Edward Arnold & Co., 1949 (1927).

Collected Short Stories. London: Penguin Books, 1954 (*The Celestial Omnibus and Other Stories*, 1911; *The Eternal Moment and Other Stories*, 1928).

England's Pleasant Land: A Pageant Play. London: The Hogarth Press, 1940.

Goldsworthy Lowes Dickenson. London: Edward Arnold & Co., 1962 (1934).

The Hill of Devi. New York: Harcourt, Brace & Co., 1953.

Howards End. London: Edward Arnold & Co., 1947 (1910).

The Longest Journey. London: Edward Arnold & Co., 1947 (1907).

Marianne Thornton: A Domestic Biography, 1797–1887. New York: Harcourt, Brace & Co., 1956.

A Passage to India. London: Edward Arnold & Co., 1947 (1924).

Pharos and Pharillon. 3rd ed. London: The Hogarth Press, 1961 (1923).

A Room with a View. London: Edward Arnold & Co., 1947 (1908).

Two Cheers for Democracy. New York: Harcourt, Brace & Co., 1951.

Where Angels Fear to Tread. London: Edward Arnold & Co., 1947 (1905).

A SELECTION OF UNCOLLECTED MATERIAL

"Albergo Empedocle," *Temple Bar*, CXXVIII (December, 1903), 663–84.

"Arctic Summer" (Fragment of an Unfinished Novel). *Tribute to Benjamin Britten on His Fiftieth Birthday*. ed. by Anthony Gishford. London: Faber & Faber, 1963, pp. 46–55.

"Author's Notes," *A Passage to India*. London: J. M. Dent and Sons, 1957, pp. xxix–xxx.

"The Blue Boy," *The Listener*, LVII (March 14, 1957), 444.

"Dante," *The Working Men's College Journal*, x (February, 1908), 261–64; x (March, 1908), 281–86; x (April, 1908), 301–06.

"De Senectute," *The London Magazine*, IV (November, 1957), 15–18.

"Erotic Indian Sculpture," *The Listener*, LXI (March 12, 1959) 469–71.

"Fog Over Ferney," *The Listener*, LX (December 18, 1958), 1029–1030.

The Government of Egypt. London: Labour Research Department, 1920, pp. 3–12 and *passim*.

"A Great Humanist," *The Listener*, LVI (October 11, 1956), 545–547.

"Indian Entries," *Encounter*, XVIII (January, 1962), 20–27.

"Introduction," *Collected Short Stories*. London: Penguin Books, 1954 (1947), pp. 5–7.

"Introduction," *The Longest Journey*. London: Oxford University Press, 1960, pp. ix–xiv.

"Introduction," *The Warm Country*, by Donald Windham. New York: Charles Scribner's Sons, 1960.

"A Letter," *The Twentieth Century*, XLVII (February, 1955), 99–101.

"Letters," in *Letters to T. E. Lawrence*. ed. by A. W. Lawrence. London: Jonathan Cape, 1962, pp. 58–75.

"Nordic Twilight," *England Speaks: A Symposium*. New York: The Macmillan Co., 1941 (1940).

"Notes," *A Passage to India* ("Everyman's Library"). London: J. M. Dent & Sons, 1957.

"Pessimism in Literature," *The Working Men's College Journal*. x (January, 1907), 6–10; x (February, 1907), 26–33.

"Recollections of Nassenheide," *The Listener*, LXI (January 1, 1959), 12–14.

"Tourism v. Thuggism," *The Listener*, LVII (January 17, 1957), 124.

"A View Without A Room," *The New York Times Book Review*, July 27, 1958, p. 4.

SOME INTERVIEWS OF E M. FORSTER

Furbank, P. N., and Haskell, F. J. H. "E. M. Forster," *Writers at Work: The Paris Review Interviews*, ed. Malcolm Cowley. New York: The Viking Press, 1959, pp. 25–35.

Gransden, K. W. "E. M. Forster at Eighty," *Encounter*, XII (January, 1959), 77–81.

Jones, David. "E. M. Forster on his Life and his Books," *The Listener*, LXI (January 1, 1959), 11–12.

O'Connor, William Van. "A Visit with E. M. Forster," *Western Review*, XIX (Spring, 1955), 215–19.

Wilson, Angus. "A Conversation with E. M. Forster," *Encounter*, IX (November, 1957) 52–57.

WORKS ON E. M. FORSTER

Books

Beer, J. B. *The Achievement of E. M. Forster*. London: Chatto & Windus, 1962.

Brown, E. K. *Rhythm in the Novel*. Toronto: University of Toronto Press, 1950.

Crews, F. C. *E. M. Forster: The Perils of Humanism*. Princeton, N. J.: Princeton University Press, 1962.

Gransden, K. W. *E. M. Forster*. New York: Grove Press, 1962.

Joseph, David I. *The Art of Rearrangement: E. M. Forster's Abinger Harvest.* New Haven: Yale University Press, 1964.

Kirkpatrick, B. J. *A Bibliography of E. M. Forster.* London: Rupert Hart-Davis, 1965.

McConkey, James. *The Novels of E. M. Forster.* Ithaca: Cornell University Press, 1957.

Macaulay, Rose. *The Writings of E. M. Forster.* London: The Hogarth Press, 1938.

Moore, Harry T. *E. M. Forster.* New York: Columbia University Press, 1965.

Natwar-Singh, K. *E. M. Forster: A Tribute. With Selections from His Writings on India.* New York: Harcourt, Brace & World, 1964.

Oliver, H. J. *The Art of E. M. Forster.* London: Melbourne University Press, 1960.

Shusterman, David. *The Quest for Certitude in E. M. Forster's Fiction.* Bloomington: Indiana University Press, 1966.

Stone, Wilfred. *The Cave and the Mountain: A Study of E. M. Forster.* Stanford: Stanford University Press, 1966.

Trilling, Lionel. *E. M. Forster.* London: The Hogarth Press, 1944 (1943).

Warner, Rex. *E. M. Forster.* Published for the British Council and the National Book League by Longmans, Green & Company, 1950.

Wilde, Alan. *Art and Order: A Study of E. M. Forster.* New York: New York University Press, 1964.

Selected Articles on E. M. Forster

Allen, Walter. "Reassessments—*Howards End*," *New Statesman and Nation*, XLIX (March 19, 1965), 407–8.

Annan, Noel. "E. M. Forster," *New Statesman and Nation*, XXVIII (October 7, 1944), 239–40.

Ault, Peter. "Aspects of E. M. Forster," *The Dublin Review*, CCXIX (October, 1946), 109–34.

Belgion, Montgomery. "The Diabolism of Mr. E. M. Forster," *Criterion*, XIV (October, 1934), 54–73.

Bowen, Elizabeth. *Collected Impressions.* New York: Alfred Knopf, 1950, pp. 119–26.

Brower, Reuben A. "Beyond E. M. Forster: Part 1—The Earth." *Foreground*, I (Spring–Summer, 1946), 164–74.

————. "Beyond E. M. Forster: The Unseen," *The Chicago Review*, II (Fall–Winter, 1948), 102–12.

Burra, Peter. "Introduction," *A Passage to India* ("Everyman's Library"). London: J. M. Dent & Sons, 1957, pp. xi–xxviii.

Cecil, David. *Poets and Story Tellers*. London: Constable & Co., 1949, pp. 181–201.

Connolly, Cyril. *The Condemned Playground: Essays, 1927–1944*. New York: The Macmillan Co., 1946, pp. 254–59 and *passim*.

———— *Enemies of Promise*. Revised ed. London: Macmillan and Co., 1949, pp. 26–27.

Cox, C. B. *The Free Spirit*. London: Oxford University Press, 1963, pp. 74–102 and *passim*.

Dobrée, Bonamy. *The Lamp and the Lute: Studies in Six Modern Authors*. 2nd ed. London: Frank Cass & Co., 1964, pp. 65–81.

Fuller, John. "E. M. Forster at Seventy," *Adelphi*, XXVIII (May, 1952), 592–93.

Fussell, Paul, Jr. "E. M. Forster's Mrs. Moore: Some Suggestions," *Philological Quarterly*, XXXII (October, 1953), 388–95.

Gerber, Helmut E. "E. M. Forster: An Annotated Checklist of Writings About Him," *English Fiction in Transition*, II (Spring, 1959), 4–27.

Grubb, Frederick. "Homage to E. M. Forster," *Contemporary Review*, No. 1117 (January, 1959), 20–23.

Hall, James. "Forster's Family Reunions," *English Literary History*, XXV (March, 1958), 60–78.

Harvey, John. "Imagination and Moral Theme in E. M. Forster's *The Longest Journey*," *Essays in Criticism*, VI, (October 1956), 418–33.

Holt, Lee Elbert. "E. M. Forster and Samuel Butler," *PMLA*, LXI (September, 1946) 804–19.

Hoy, Cyrus. "Forster's Metaphysical Novel," *PMLA*, LXXV, (March, 1960), 123–36.

Johnson, E. H. "The Intelligent Mr. E. M. Forster," *Personalist*, XXXV (January, 1954), 50–58.

Johnstone, J. K. "E. M. Forster," *The Bloomsbury Group: A Study of E. M. Forster, Lytton Strachey, Virginia Woolf, and Their Circle*. New York: The Noonday Press, 1954, pp. 159–266.

Karl, Frederick R., and Marvin Magalaner. *A Reader's Guide* to *Great Twentieth-Century English Novels.* New York: Noonday Press, 1959, pp. 100–124.

Kermode, Frank. "Mr. E. M. Forster as a Symbolist," *The Listener,* LIX (January 2, 1958), 17–18.

Kettle, Arnold. *An Introduction to the English Novel.* Vol. II, London: Hutchinson & Co., 1951, pp. 152–63.

Lawrence, D. H. *Letters.* ed. by Harry T. Moore. 2 vols. New York: Viking Press, 1962. pp. 315, 316, 317–18, 323, 716, 793, 799, 800, 811, 1024, 1124.

Leavis, F. R., "E. M. Forster," *The Common Pursuit.* Peregrine Books. Harmondsworth, Middlesex, England: Penguin Books, 1962, pp. 261–77.

———— "Meet Mr. Forster," *Scrutiny,* XII (Autumn, 1944), 308–309.

McConkey, James. "The Voice of the Writer," *University of Kansas City Review,* XXV (December, 1958) 83–90.

McDowell, Frederick P. W. "The Mild Intellectual Light: Idea and Theme in *Howards End,*" *PMLA,* LXXIV (September, 1959), 453–63.

McLuhan, Herbert Marshall. "Kipling and Forster," *Sewanee Review,* LII (Summer, 1944), 332–42.

Macdonald, Alastair. "Class Consciousness in E. M. Forster," *University of Kansas City Review,* XXVII (Spring, 1961), 235–40.

Maclean, Hugh. "The Structure of *A Passage to India,*" *University of Toronto Quarterly,* XXII (January, 1953), 157–71.

Modern Fiction Studies. E. M. Forster Number, VII (Autumn, 1961). Contains articles by Alan Wilde, Louise Dauner, Frederick J. Hoffman, Frederick P. W. McDowell, George H. Thomson, and Don Austin. Contains also a selected checklist of criticism of E. M. Forster's work.

Painter-Downes, Mollie. "Profiles: Kingsman," *The New Yorker,* XXXV (September 19, 1959), 51–86.

Pederson, Glenn. "Forster's Symbolic Form," *Kenyon Review,* XXI (Spring, 1959), 231–49.

Priestley, J. B. "Review of *A Passage to India, The London Mercury,* v. 10 (July, 1924), 319–20.

Pritchett, V. S. "Mr. Forster's New Year," *New Statesman and Nation,* LVI (December 27, 1958), 912–13.

Richards, I. A. "A Passage to Forster: Reflections on a Novelist," *Forum,* LXXVIII (December, 1927), 914–20.

Ransom, John Crowe. "E. M. Forster," *Kenyon Review,* v (Autumn, 1943), 618–23.

Savage, D. S. *The Withered Branch: Six Studies in the Modern Novel.* London: Eyre & Spottiswoode, 1950, pp. 44–69.

Shanks, Edward. "Mr. E. M. Forster," *London Mercury,* xvi (July, 1927) 265–74.

Shusterman, David. "The Curious Case of Professor Godbole: *A Passage to India* Re-examined," *PMLA,* lxxvi (September, 1961), 426–35.

Shipley, John B. "Additions to the E. M. Forster Bibliography," *The Papers of the Bibliographical Society of America,* lx (First Quarter, 1966), pp. 224–25.

Spence, Jonathan. "E. M. Forster at Eighty," *New Republic,* cxli (October 5, 1959), 17–21.

Stevenson, Lionel. *The English Novel: A Panorama.* Boston: Houghton Mifflin, 1960, pp. 453, 462, 472, 476, 515, 532.

Traversi, D. A. "The Novels of E. M. Forster," *Arena,* i (April, 1937), 28–40.

Wilson, Angus. "The Revolt of Samuel Butler," *The Atlantic Monthly,* cc (November, 1957), 190–98.

Woolf, Virginia. *The Death of the Moth and Other Essays.* London: The Hogarth Press, 1942, pp. 104–12.

——— *The Moment and Other Essays.* New York: Harcourt, Brace & Co., 1948, pp. 89–93.

Zabel, Morton Dauwen. *Craft and Character in Modern Fiction.* New York: The Viking Press, 1957, pp. 228–52.

SELECTED BOOKS ON THE THEORY OF THE NOVEL

Booth, Wayne C. *The Rhetoric of Fiction.* Chicago: University of Chicago Press, 1961.

Lubbock, Percy. *The Craft of Fiction.* Compass Books Edition, New York: The Viking Press, 1957 (1921).

INDEX